Oh Boy
Oh Boy
Oh Boy!

Confronting
Motherhood,
Womanhood
& Selfhood in
a Household
of Boys

"I never thought anyone could capture the true spirit of my son—ALL of our sons—on paper. Yet Karin Kasdin does it with amazing accuracy and disarming humor. Karin proves that motherhood truly is one twenty-four-hour sit-com!"

DANA FLEMING, Host,
"Kids These Days,"
Lifetime Television

Oh Boy
Oh Boy
Oh Boy!

*Confronting
Motherhood,
Womanhood
& Selfhood in
a Household
of Boys*

Karin Kasdin

SIBYL
PUBLICATIONS
Portland, Oregon

Published by SIBYL Publications, Inc. • 1007 S.W. Westwood Drive •
Portland, Oregon 97201 • (503) 293-8391 • 800-240-8566

Copyright © 1997 Karin Kasdin

ISBN 0-9638327-9-4

Editor: *Marge Columbus*

Graphic Design: *Design Studio Selby*

6 5 4 3 2 1

Cataloging in Publication Data

Kasdin, Karin.
    Oh boy. Oh boy. Oh boy! : confronting motherhood, woman-
hood & selfhood in a household of boys / Karin Kasdin. -- 1st ed.
    p. cm.
    ISBN: 0-9638327-9-4

    1. Kasdin, Karin. 2. Motherhood--United States--Anecdotes.
3. Mothers and sons--United States--Biography. I. Title.

HQ759.K38 1997   306.874'3'092
                                        QBI97-40571

Printed in the United States of America

Contents

Introduction 1

It's a Boy! Again. 5

To Cut or Not to Cut 12

The Boys' Department 17

Midlife Baseball 26

I Menstruate. They Don't. 31

Me Want Car 35

Does That Grunt Mean Hello? 40

Letting Hoppy Go 46

Belching, Farting, and
Other Table Manners 52

Boys' Noise 58

Advice and Sex 63

Gun of a Son 71

Good Night, Zack 77

Night Thoughts 82

Morning's Come Up 85

Getting Ready 88

A Hole in One ... Ear 91

20 Things to Do in Synagogue
Besides Participate 96

My Loves Are Blind 102

Home Is Where the Mess Is 107

Thoughts vs. Feelings 116

He Ain't Heavy,
He's My Little Brother 122

Louisa May Who? 128

I Can Do Anything Better
Than You. And I Do. 136

More Night Thoughts 141

Male-Nutrition 143

Lookin' Good 145

The Naked Truth 150

Kimmy 155

Now You See It …
Now You Still See It 159

If No Means No and Maybe
Means No, What Does
Yes Mean? Maybe No. 164

Sons of the Beach 168

Solitary Confinement
as Fact of Life 173

The Importance of Being Dad 178

Bashing Bashing 181

Epilogue 184

About the Author 187

For the men in my life, from A to Z,
who have brought me boundless joy,
and who have made it possible for me
to write, out of love, a book about men:

Albert, Andrew, Daniel, Harold, Irwin,
Jeremy, Louis, and Zack.

But especially for Harold, my partner
in passion and parenthood.

Acknowledgments

With love and gratitude I acknowledge:

Sarah Jane Freymann for all of her efforts on my behalf.

Carolyn Tilove for helping me to find, love, and nurture the girl-child in me.

My newest friend, James Andrew Miller, who forced me to focus, and whose astute advice and generous encouragement helped me turn a corner.

My beloved intimate circle, Edye Kamensky, Amy Levine, and Elayne Klein, for listening with love and laughter and lunch.

My brilliant partner and friend of friends, Laura Szabo Cohen, who took more phone calls from me than there are words in this book, whose wit and wisdom I cherish, and whose confidence in me is steadfast on even my most uninspired days.

My mother, Phyllis, whose infinite love made it natural for me to want to mother, and to my other mother, Marilyn, who miraculously raised the enlightened man I love before feminism even had a name.

And my sons, Daniel, Andrew, and Zack, for allowing their souls to be dissected in wonder, in humor, in frustration, and in deepest, purest love. Thank you for the gift of you.

Introduction

I believe in sisterhood. When my reproductive instincts self-activated at the age of twenty-seven, I ached with every cell in my body to bring a confident and courageous daughter into the fold. I knew on a molecular level that I would be a wonderful mother to a girl. I had been a girl. Could it be any more challenging to raise one than to be one? My mother, the woman whose counsel I have always treasured, had been a girl and had raised two girls. Finding wise and loving support would not have been an obstacle. Ten years and three children later, when I finally posted the "gone fishin' " sign on my uterus, I unexpectedly found five free minutes one day, and I used them to take stock of the bountiful blessings God had bestowed upon me. A daughter was not among them. I had been granted the gift of three bouncing boys. As I begin this diary of lessons learned and foibles recounted, my oldest son, Dan, is thirteen and still bouncing. Andrew, my middle son, is ten, and Zack, my baby, who isn't a baby any more but will be to me for the rest of my life, is three. I love them with every cell in my body and I know they love me in ways that are clear to them now and in ways they have yet to discover. I don't always understand them and they don't always understand me, and we sometimes fumble along in a thick fog, but our hands and our hearts are linked as we find our way together.

They wonder why my feelings are so easily hurt, and I wonder why they don't understand that they're often the cause. I know I'm from Venus and they're from Mars. I know they *Just Don't Understand* about the *Backlash*. But knowing and knowing *what to do* are different things entirely.

This is not a book of advice. Nor is it the culmination of exhaustive scientific research on the efficacy of various child-rearing techniques on boys. I have no tips. But I have many sons. And no daughters. While having one son is indeed a challenge, it is the interaction *between* boys that accounts for the holes in the wallpaper and your colon.

This book is my way of sharing my reality with other women, my effort to bond with mothers who have been equally blessed and challenged. It is the story of a journey still in progress, of successes and failures, of epiphanies and of mysteries that may never be solved. I am writing *my* truth about raising sons as I experience each glory and each disappointment. The timbre of this work may vary from topic to topic regardless of the rule that a book stay true to its intended tone. My reality includes mood swings. Giant leaps from elation to despair and back. Sometimes. Other times things get dreadfully dull. That is truth number one about mothering children of either gender.

My girlfriend Laura says that the love a mother feels for her sons is a miracle. I think she's right. It is natural for a woman to love a girlbaby with whom she shares a place in history and culture and biology. But to love so much that you would be willing to die for beings so vastly different from yourself is nothing short of miraculous. And it happens all the time. It happened to me. I show my sons (the two who can read) each of these chapters as I create them. They have no objections. They are not insulted. They are proud that I want to write about them—even if it means I must tell the truth. This book is my gift to them, to my sisters who are also the mothers of sons, and to all women who have ever loved or been amazed by somebody's son.

There are mothers I've met who have never wanted daughters. Mothers who harbor no secret pinings for canopy beds or pink hair ribbons or sweet sixteen parties. God bless them. And God bless my sons. Even though there ...

It's a Boy! Again.

There are certain thoughts a mother wouldn't dare utter out loud for fear that God will either smite her children or bestow upon them untold wealth and happiness, causing them to relocate to Malibu so she can live out the rest of her days in natural disaster panic. Among these unspeakable epithets are: "Fuck you, you little shit," " I wish I never had children," and (if you're speaking to a boy) "I wish you had been born a girl."

I believe in God. I believe that God is a mother. Which is why, even though I would never ever say the nasty little quips I listed above, I have no problem saying that I think them. On occasion. Mother God will understand. I've met some of her children. You can't convince me that on occasion she doesn't stifle a put-down or two. So, because I truly believed she would understand my evil thoughts and not punish me for having them as long as I *never ever* shared them with my boys, I was surprisingly guilt-free about admitting to select friends and my ob-gyn that I was disappointed when the results of my amniocentesis indicated that my third and last child would be a third and last boy. I think I even said "shit" to my doctor. She'd heard it before.

I had assured my husband, Harold, before we even assembled the ingredients that I was not making this baby because I desperately wanted a girl, but because I desperately wanted a BABY. I had lied. What I desperately wanted was another vagina in the house. I wanted a lifetime soul sister— someone who would appreciate *Pride and Prejudice* and a great *mille-feuille* and Paul Newman. I was immune to the reptilian charms of the Ninja Turtles. I wanted a dollhouse.

So I read the recipe for making a girl. It's uncanny how similar it is to the Cordon Bleu School's recipe for coulibiac of salmon. Practically impossible in every way. The odds for success are completely stacked against you. First you have to find the time. Good luck. Then you have to use ingredients that you've never seen before and probably couldn't find in your neighborhood even if your cooking encyclopedia had a color photo. The mousse must always be on top of the salmon and not the other way around or the phyllo cloak will tear, and the champagne will cause the sauce to curdle unless you heat it to within three degrees of perfection, which you have to estimate by determining how far you live from the Equator or Greenwich, England, I can't remember which. If you manage to complete the process without committing suicide or heinous abominations to the salmon, the coulibiac will be museum quality art on a plate. Three percent of the time. The other ninety-seven percent of the time it will be fish hash.

Little X chromosomes peek out only a few times a month. They are partial to an acidic environment, a splash of vinegar in the mix. They are small and delicate and they slip out easily, so you must make sure you are on the bottom every time, and you must keep your feet up for twelve minutes afterward and not think or talk about Newt Gingrich for four days after each encounter. If you meticulously follow each directive, you are guaranteed to make a girl. Three percent of the time. Fifty percent of the time you will make a girl anyway even if you screw up screwing. The other fifty percent of the time it will be *Boystown* for you. Our love life became routine and complicated and anything but romantic, but we did it by the book. Many times. Father Flanagan must have been watching.

So hate me if you want—call me an ungrateful bitch for not being so overjoyed at the news that my baby was healthy that all thoughts of gender instantly disintegrated. Report me to Phyllis Schlafly. I was disappointed. For a day. Okay, for two days. Okay, for the whole rest of the pregnancy until the moment I saw his sweet face and knew that loving him would be easier and more natural than breathing. From the moment his baby-blue slightly underoxygenated body metamorphosed into pink, I have not experienced one second of disappointment that I bore him. Just as I've never been disappointed about creating his brothers. It is impossible for me to regret having a child. It is only possible to regret not having one. Which is why, even as I nestled my new love in my grateful arms, I found it necessary to mourn for my daughter.

I was too racked with emotion and overcome with fatigue to search my heart for the source of my self-inflicted lamentations. Now, three years and one therapist later, I ask myself what it was exactly that caused me to grieve. I close my eyes and I open my soul and my hands begin to move in smooth, over and under waves of motion. I know that I am weaving braids. Over the past thirteen years (fourteen now as I edit the final draft of this manuscript) I've bathed babies and nursed babies and helped kids tie shoes and tie ties and apply pimple cream, but I've never braided my child's hair. The simple physical act of braiding hair is universal and primordial. It links women to each other regardless of race, color, religion, or historical milieu. Moses' sister Miriam wore braids (according to Cecil B. DeMille anyway). Ancient Greek women wore braids. Diana, goddess of the hunt, had them. Chinese mothers did and do braid their daughters' hair as do Native American mothers and African mothers and European mothers and Laura Ingalls's mother. The act of braiding a daughter's hair seems to me to be an intimacy one can never parallel with one's male children. I have shared exquisite moments of intimacy with my boys. Moments that are the jewels I will be bedecked in when I'm buried. These moments bind me to them inextricably and eternally, but not globally or historically. I mourned the nonexistence of the child who would have linked me to the women who have come before me in my own family and in the family of all women.

There is something healthy about mourning the loss of a

child you longed for but never had. I feel better now that I've done it. I have boundless compassion for women who miscarry. Their pain must be devastating because they mourn for the possible. My pain was different. Less excruciating to be sure, but to me, no less real. I mourned for a child I had only imagined. She had never been possible. She had never been so much as a zygote. But I knew her essence, and I loved her. Every now and then, usually after a friend tells me about a particularly intimate mother-daughter experience, I find myself mourning for her again, and the process always makes me hungry for lobster salad.

Every September, at the start of the new school year, my mother would take me shopping for school clothes. We'd get dressed up and drive downtown to the big new indoor mall, where I would hold her hand extra tight to avoid being swept into the battalions of blue-suited men on lunch break, or the several thousand other suburban mother-daughter shopping teams on expedition. I think one of my old friends still shops there. For combat boots. The place is a war zone now, but to a nine-year-old girl in 1964 it was as romantic as Casablanca. Halfway through our shopping trip, Mom would take me to the seventh floor of a now defunct department store, where we would order the most glorious lobster salad sandwiches for lunch. We couldn't eat lobster at home because my mother maintained a strictly kosher kitchen. Our little forays into "trafedom" (eating of nonkosher food) were mutually gratifying little sins.

No one can whip up a simple four-course dinner like my mother can. I once saw her bake and serve ten kinds of pie at one meal just because she could. The fact that there were only six of us at the table was irrelevant to her. As savory as her cooking was, however, I never relished anything she concocted as much as I did those annual lobster salad sandwiches. They tasted of indulgence and intimacy and collusion. Thirty years later I think of them and am reminded of purple corduroy miniskirts and white go-go boots. Lobster salad signifies for me—more than the most brilliant crimson and gold—autumn.

I don't keep a kosher home. It's not a sin for me to eat anything (except white bread, which Laura's son told me has sawdust in it). Still, even sans the element of sin, I'm sure I could find a foodstuff that would come to mean autumn to a little girl. I mourned the loss of the chance to do that. My boys hate shopping and eat pizza only, which, if I saved for a once-a-year treat, would, to them, justify matricide.

I mourned for myself and I mourned for my boys because they wouldn't have a sister to grow up with. I have much I want to teach them about equality and respect for gender differences. I want to share my lofty ideals about mutual support and admiration and respect between the sexes. Showing is so much better than telling. And all I can do is tell. It's as if I've designed the best transparencies in the world, but the bulb blew out in the overhead projector. My sons can feel the high regard in which my husband and I hold each other. Big deal. We're grown-ups. It's our job to set a good example. Having a sister would have been a more organic way for them to evolve.

I have voiced the unspeakable. I wanted a daughter and I was sad for awhile that I wasn't granted one. Now and then I am still sad. Judging from the mothers of sons with whom I have shared my feelings, the unspeakable is spoken all the time. Silently. It is what women do best. We say "How dare you?" to ourselves for wanting more when we've already been endowed with the world. For years I was certain that God would punish me for my daughter cravings by bringing harm to one of the sons I adore. *PU-LEASE!* I never said I'd consider trading one of them in or anything. I wanted a girl *too*. Each of us has the right to ask for as much as we want. God doesn't measure that which she bestows upon us. Unfortunately, she also doesn't measure that which she chooses to deny. So ask. And accept thankfully and graciously. And ask for some more. And keep on accepting. But while you're accepting, learn to accept rejection. It helps with the mourning process. Does that count as advice? Oops.

To Cut or Not to Cut

Aside from the female bonding matter, I had another valid reason for my disappointment when the amnio indicated the presence of a little penis. It was the knowledge of what was going to happen to that little penis exactly eight days after birth. I had been through it twice before. You don't get stronger each time. Only your tranquilizers do.

I know it's not castration, but I couldn't have felt worse if that's what it had been. No one forced me to go through with it, but on a primeval level, I knew I would suffer five thousand years of ancestral wrath if I opted out.

I haven't read any recent statistics, but I'm fairly certain that the majority of male babies in this country are circumcised on the day of or on the day after birth. Even if it's not a true majority, I feel safe saying that a lot of babies are circumcised and certainly almost all Jewish male babies are. The torturous thing about being the mother of a Jewish baby boy is that they make you (they being the men who decide what it was that God decided) stew for eight days prior to the event, and they make you (they being the first caterers ever to put mayo to whitefish) celebrate with a brunch. Or a late afternoon repast if the moyel (one who circumcises) has three scheduled cuttings before yours that day.

Preparing for a bris is not like planning any other kind of life cycle event, except for the coffee and buffet part. You worry about things far less trivial than which of your great-aunts is deaf enough to sit next to the orchestra. For example, I took one look at our second son's moyel and was convinced that he was suffering from Parkinson's disease. It didn't make me think any less of him as a person. Unfortunate and unavoidable things like that start happening to you when you get to be about a hundred. I believe strongly in equal opportunity for the old and infirm, but not when the opportunity involves my precious baby, a trembling hand, and a blade.

Anesthesia was another concern. Why didn't my babies get any? They were given two sips of Manischewitz Concord Grape Wine. That's not anesthesia. That's dessert.

Witnessing a circumcision is not something that gets easier with experience, like wiping up pizza vomit. Mothers can never desensitize themselves to their children's pain. The moyel invariably makes a feeble attempt to comfort the mother by assuring her in his most soothing voice that the procedure isn't painful because it happens so fast. This is a lie. I know that cutting a baby's penis hurts the baby the same way I know that boiling a live lobster hurts the lobster. I can tell by the screaming. I never went to medical school, but it seems to me that screaming is a fairly accurate indicator of pain. Generally, my babies don't scream unless something is upsetting them beyond their ability to cope. Whimper and whine, they do ... but they don't scream without due cause. Until they're two. Then they don't stop screaming for a year and a half. After his bris, my oldest screamed for five minutes, nursed for two hours, and slept for three days. My middle son screamed for three days and experienced a complete and permanent personality change. Prior to the foreskin removal he was docile and content. Afterward and to this day he doesn't know what he wants, but he's sure that whatever he has isn't it.

I don't remember how son number three reacted. By then I had learned to meditate, while drinking Manischewitz and humming obscure Yoko Ono tunes. I remember we had hardly any whitefish left, which must mean that people weren't too depressed or sick to their stomachs to eat.

What I want to know is this: if God is indeed a mother, how do you account for circumcision? Even if she's a Jewish mother, you can explain the food part, but the procedure is still unconscionable. Why didn't she just create penises the way she wanted them to look in the first place?

Circumcision apparently was a more sanitary alternative to the au naturel option back in pre-stall-shower days. I suppose a circumcised penis is still easier to clean than one which has retained its foreskin. If my sons had to be responsible for a body part that required more than a casual wipe now and then, they would all be eunuchs by their Bar Mitzvahs. Dry rot would surely set in within a year or two after I'd stop bathing them myself. Grown-up men could probably meet the hygiene challenge, but for them it would be too late.

I often wonder about the victim aspect of the circumcision experience—the Captain Hook Effect. According to the Peter Pan story, Captain Hook's hand was bitten off by a crocodile when he was a young boy. Following that gruesome experience he became the bitter, arrogant, aggressive character whom readers and audiences have loved to hate for decades. And he merely lost a hand. His crown jewels were left intact. Newborns are naive, but not stupid. In whatever primordial thought process they're capable of, I'm sure each boy baby subjected to this practice swears with a justifiable vengeance never to be weak and powerless again. And who could blame him? Look at what the caretakers in his life allowed to happen to him! Unfortunately, he is now hard-wired for a lifelong pattern of arrogance and bullying. It's not pleasant, but it's one explanation for war.

I shared my theory with the Rabbi, who had this to say. "History has shown us time and again that Jewish men pick fewer fights and are generally more cerebral and less violence-prone than are men of the uncircumcised variety." Well, maybe. But if that's the case, I wish someone would explain why half of our holidays exist because a mere handful of Jewish soldiers were able to decimate the entire Roman, Greek (Insert the nation of your choice, we've had to fight them all) army? Don't get me wrong. I'm glad they won. I like the fact that my people survived so I could be born. And aesthetically I prefer the "clipped" style. But, if I had a body part cut off of me for no comprehensible reason, I might take the same "Make my day" stand. What I won't do is ever watch a bris again. Without anesthesia.

The Boys' Department

Shopping for Boys

I've already written about shopping when I discussed those lobster salad sandwich excursions, so I know I run the risk of being thought of as an addle-brained shop-a-holic if I pursue the subject, but I can't help it. When a woman has a baby, she can't wait to cuddle it, nurse it, and shop for it. With few exceptions, girls begin dressing babies even before they develop the fine motor skills necessary to the task. I warmly remember fumbling with the buttons on my Chatty Cathy's pink floral pajamas. I still *have* my Chatty Cathy doll *and* her pink floral pajamas. She sits desperate for the love of a little girl on the shelf above my desk, where she is safe from the hands of maniac boys who would love a chance to eviscerate her to figure out how her voicebox works.

I can call to mind every outfit Shirley Temple ever wore— her *Heidi* lederhosen, her *Rebecca of Sunnybrook Farm* gingham, and of course her most luscious of all *Little Miss Broadway* fur-trimmed coat and hat set that I knew was red even though her movies were in black and white. I would have kissed Barney Fyfe for that outfit. As the years passed I eagerly awaited the chance to shop *for* a little girl and then to shop *with* a little girl.

While pregnant for the first time, I would unconsciously veer from the maternity area to the infant department and head straight for the pink. Having been born well before Molly Ringwald made it possible for redheads to be pretty in pink, I was denied that fashion option throughout my formative years. Now I lingered dreamily amidst the pink nighties and hair ribbons and ruffled socks.

I was born on the eve of Saint Patrick's Day, and befitting the impending holiday, it was obvious to all present that the stork had taken a wrong turn on his way to Killarney. My bonnie red hair and freckles were anomalies that cried out to be swathed in shamrock green. Had I been born an hour later, my parents planned to name me Kelly, which would have turned me for life into a walking oxymoron. I managed to beat the clock and was given an American name with a Scandinavian spelling. That being accomplished, I was washed up and bundled into a green receiving blanket. I must have looked delicious because my mother dressed me like a zucchini for the next ten years.

I had different fashion plans for my baby. My daughter-to-be, born of a dark father, would reflect her Eastern European Jewish heritage in her dark eyes and ebony hair. She would wear Jackie Kennedy pink to perfection.

Dan could never have pulled off Jackie Kennedy pink. It clashes with Lucy Ricardo red. Not only was he a boy, but he, like me, had a leprechaun's countenance. My first trip to the baby shop was not quite as I had imagined it would be.

Bypassing the ruffles and matching ponytail holders and black patent leather Mary Janes, I found myself in a maze of clothes with soccer balls and trucks and tools embroidered, embossed, or painted on them. It was as if my son was being coached from beyond on whom and what to be from the time he wore a size zero-three months. What if he didn't like soccer? What if he liked reading? Or botany? Where were the shirts with the sequoias on them? Baby girls were allowed to wear plaid and checks and polka dots. Boys had to wear hobbies. Or they could dress like girls. The generic, hobby-free boy baby clothes were prissy. Some even came with berets. I wasn't interested in having a tiny Marcel Marceau in the house. I bought a wee pair of jeans and some hobby shirts. What choice did I have? I did my best to make Dan look adorable. Fortunately, he didn't require any help. But when it came time to preen ourselves for a trip to Grandma's or a holiday dinner, I confess to major bouts of fashion envy when my nieces arrived sporting bloomers with lace that matched their collars and anklets, and my son was wearing a new green shirt that looked an awful lot like his old green shirt. I'm not proud of such petty self-pity. I can only plead immaturity. That was thirteen and a half years ago. Today little boy babies don't have to wear hobbies on their chests unless their mommies insist. Today mommies can dress little boys in shirts that simply say GAP or OLD NAVY as if that actually means something. Unfortunately, you still wouldn't want to dress your son in a beautiful red fur-trimmed coat and hat set.

Shopping with Boys

The fact that not one of my boys was physically able to sit in a stroller for more than a minute and a half at a stretch should have clued me in early on that they would be woefully inadequate shopping companions. Still, twice a year I let myself imagine a shopping spree during which we would share our views of the world while combing the racks at our favorite department store. My sons have never exhibited any interest whatsoever in combing the racks. They have always preferred hiding under the racks so as to let the newest look in sleeves or pantlegs tickle their noses. A favorite game of Dan's was "Let's see how high I can count before Mom notices that I'm missing and starts to convulse." We've all heard our share of "Monster in the Mall" stories—shockers about evil people who can abduct a child in three and a half seconds, have the tyke's hair dyed in two minutes, and waltz out the door unnoticed before Mom even realizes that her child has let go of her hand. I believe that a moment's embarrassment is preferable to a lifetime of anguish, so shy as I am, I never hesitated to scream my bloody head off when I suspected that one of my children was lost. I'm astounded that my local Macy's hasn't suspended my shopping privileges. Harold could never understand why I neglected to look for the boys under the racks, when that was where they were each time I misplaced them. Go explain brain paralysis to a father who hears the story only after the happy ending. Only another mother can understand the instantaneous coma you fall into the nanosecond you suspect that your child is missing. By my calculation I should've been dead forty-seven times by now.

It takes a while to recover from the gut fear that your child may be lying in a ditch somewhere because you spent thirty seconds too long debating whether to buy his jeans with or without elastic in the back. But we mothers of sons are a hearty lot, and we never let the possibility of death or mutilation interfere with a mission involving textiles. I always managed to pull myself together after a false alarm long enough to tackle the jeans question from all angles. An elastic waist would definitely make for a more comfortable fit, but everybody knows elastic is not cool. And cool rules when you have big brothers who will eat you for lunch if you dress like a geek. I always opt for nonelasticized pants. The kind you have to try on.

My children enjoy their DPT shots more than they enjoy trying on clothes. They're too hot. They're so sweaty they'll stink up the new clothes and then we'll *have* to buy them even if we hate them. It's too hard to get their sneakers off. The lock on the dressing room door is malfunctioning. The door is too short. They're sooooo hot! Doesn't it make perfect sense just to buy one size larger than we bought the last time and call it a day? They can tell if something fits just by holding it against their bodies. They're missing their favorite television program and they're sooooooooo hot!

I could always hear the little girls in the fitting rooms on the opposite side of the children's department. They would ooh and ahh at themselves in the mirror. They would step out into the open where the saleswomen would ooh and ahh over them. Their mothers would swell with pride at the way their angels looked in their party dresses or Easter bonnets or miniature sweater sets with freshwater pearl buttons. Next Mom and child would head for the shoe department to search for the perfect patent leathers to complete the ensemble. I once suggested that we extend our shopping trip to include a stopover in the shoe department. About five years ago, I think. I know one of these days they'll get back to me on that.

To be honest, we did take our little side trips. We managed to visit the bathroom three or four times an hour each time we went shopping. I would deny them liquids on the night before a designated shopping day. To no avail. I've seen my sons sit through three hours of football while consuming a two-liter bottle of soda apiece and never once take a bathroom break. Why is it they can't spend more than twenty consecutive minutes in a retail clothing establishment without wailing that their bladders are on the verge of explosion? Bathroom jaunts are nightmares for mothers of sons. Before the age of seven or eight it is universally acceptable for little boys to use the women's room with Mom. Once they become self-conscious about anatomy differences, however, it isn't fair to embarrass big, strapping boys by forcing them to use the inappropriate lavatory. I believe the first true step toward independence is taken the first time Mommy lets her baby boy go into a public men's room by himself. I have imagined every kind of pervert hiding behind the door to hurt or fondle my little *naïf*. To make myself feel more comfortable I always insisted that Dan maintain a running conversation with me while we were apart. I would stand outside the john door and ask him how everything was coming along or what it looked like in there or if he thought the Knicks would win tonight— anything to keep the patter going until he emerged safely. He was always either safe or lying, and I always had a headache for the rest of the day.

One of the advantages of having multiple sons is that the oldest can watch the younger ones in the bathroom. I never worried about Andrew or Zack the way I did about Dan. I could relax, knowing that if the younger ones return to me in tears, it's because Dan abused them and not because some demented stranger did.

Few people are architecturally conscious enough to notice that the restrooms in department stores are typically located near the china. Mothers of sons notice. I find this architectural plan ironic, seeing as women who are shopping for china are probably the most likely of anyone in the store to be able to control their bladders. A woman with a cultivated taste for Royal Doulton would be too repulsed by public bathrooms to use them for anything other than a quick lipstick freshening. It would make far more sense to position the restrooms near the boys' department in consideration of customers who actually *use* the facility. By the time we wended our way back to the boys' department, any half-hearted attempt at motivation they might have made before trekking upstairs and back down again was now too much for them to pull off. They would grab a couple of blue shirts and a couple of pairs of black pants and beg to be set free from consumer bondage. I never knew what I was buying until I arrived home and surveyed the black and blue clumps of fabric they had thrown onto their beds.

Why can't men understand that black is black and navy is navy and they're neither interchangeable nor compatible? Dan refuses to accept the fact that you can look sharp in a black shirt with blue jeans but not in a navy shirt with black jeans. Basic denim blue is okay over black jeans, but not navy. "It's the same thing," he insists. "Blue is blue." Hardly. Andrew rejects jeans as too confining and thinks that he looks adorable in sweat pants three sizes too large. Zack would be happy to live life wearing nothing but light-up sneakers and Batman underpants. I'm not sure how to teach my sons fashion sense. Harold says it will kick in when they become interested in girls, but Harold is interested in me and he's still on the wrong side of the black-navy issue.

One day I started to shop *for* them *without* them. I wasn't exactly angry about it, just very sad. How difficult could it be,

I wondered, to feign interest in an activity that someone you love enjoys? I saw how difficult when Andrew decided he wanted to celebrate his tenth birthday by going to an Eagles game. His father was happy (well, he was willing) to comply. As for my present, Andrew wanted my presence. It was cold. I couldn't see the players because we were sitting so far away and if we had been sitting closer, I still wouldn't have been able to see them because they wear so much paraphernalia. It was cold and I don't understand the rules and I find it all to be rather barbaric anyway, not to mention boring, and I was *soooooo* cold. I fidgeted and I whined and I begged to be sent to the car and I don't think I made the experience as enjoyable for Andrew as it should have been because he barely spoke to me all the way home. In the silence I could hear Mr. Lord and Mr. Taylor laughing.

Now I shop for the boys while they're at school or at football games. I've learned that some things, despite good intentions and profound love, are impossible to do. I don't understand their inability to browse, but I accept it. I set aside four days per year to outfit my sons. I purchase three times more than they need, prepared to return to the mall the next day with the rejected items. At home they can gag and refuse to try things on and whine and hide without humiliating me. And when they resort to these tactics, I can send them to their rooms. And while they're in their rooms, they have nothing better to do so they might as well try on clothes.

Midlife Baseball

Baseball is a different matter entirely. I'd happily sacrifice an afternoon of shopping for a seat in the sun at a baseball game—well maybe not if I was gallery hopping in Soho, but definitely if I was just scoping out Banana Republic. Baseball is a gift my sons have given to me for which I will be forever grateful. Prior to having children, this is what I knew about baseball. Marilyn Monroe was once married to Joe DeMaggio and he loved her very much and still puts roses on her grave. Also I saw *Damn Yankees* on TV when I was ten and got a kick out of the fact that My Favorite Martian was the devil.

Harold knew even less than I did about the game. When our sons were born, it didn't occur to us to buy Yankees crib sheets or a stuffed Philly Phanatic. (We live halfway between New York and Philadelphia.) We were more inclined to buy Itzhak Perlman sheets and a Ben Franklin doll. The boys' rooms, their closets, indeed their infancies were smoke-, sugar- and sport-free. Nevertheless, the first two grew to be card-swapping, cap-wearing, ESPN-watching, memorabilia-collecting, stat-quoting, gum-chewing baseball fanatics. I became a foreigner in my own home—still the queen, but my subjects were definitely, God forbid, developing minds and interests of their own. Revolution in our right-brain-dominated household was imminent. I had made them pariahs on the baseball field because they had never been to a real game. The air began to smell of anarchy. My husband refused an offer to coach a team. Guilt became my constant bedfellow.

I suppose I could have chosen to fight the jock-monster—squash that insidious renegade gene that ruthlessly invaded my defenseless embryos years before. But my reserves of energy were depleted from defending Jimmy Carter. I chose instead to join them—learn the language—attend the games. I figured that my participation in baseball would be worth at least three visits to the nursing home in years to come.

The language was a snap. If you can learn Portuguese in your sleep by listening to tapes, you can't help but learn Baseball when it is screamed two inches from your face twelve hours a day. My first game (Phillies vs. Padres) would be the real challenge, and seeing as how I had flunked football so miserably, I decided to make it up to Andrew by meeting the challenge head on and with one hell of a positive attitude. I bought Phillies caps for everyone. I packed grilled portobello mushroom and roasted red pepper baguette sandwiches, and we headed for I-95 at rush hour. A month later, when we finally arrived at the stadium, none of us were speaking to each other. Andrew had a swollen finger from having it jammed into the car ashtray by his loving big brother. Dan had a bald spot from Andrew pulling clumps of hair out of his head. I closed my eyes and tried to visualize a seat at the Gershwin Theater in New York. I didn't even care what was playing.

I think we sat in the ozone hole. King Kong sat in front of me. I'm sure he had beans for lunch. It was two hundred and fifty degrees. The hot dogs (Okay, I should have known they'd never eat my sandwiches) were sweaty and six dollars. I closed my eyes and tried to visualize a monsoon. By the seventh inning stretch people were fainting. No one had scored, but I was starting to recognize names. The rotund filthy one was John Kruk, the rotund hairy one was Pete Incaviglia, the rotund pitcher was—etc.

By the eighth inning I accidentally started to enjoy myself. After realizing that I couldn't catch a show even if I left that very second and got beamed to New York, I began to relax. The later it got, the cooler the temperature became. I decided to try cheering with my kids when Lenny Dykstra hit one over the fence. I groaned when Mickey Morandini struck out. I hyperventilated when Darren Daulton—showed up. My husband was impressed. King Kong actually slouched a little so I could see better. I began to scream epithets at the opposing team. No one blanched at hearing a woman swear. I was hooked.

Now I can name all of the Phillies and all of the Yankees and many of the Giants and Padres and Braves and White Sox too. Now we go to six games or more per season, and I don't even care if they have fireworks on those nights. Now I wear my Phillies cap to the park or sometimes even to the movies. Now I throw and I catch. I still can't hit. I have Darren Daulton's autograph on a program, and I don't make social engagements with friends on World Series nights. I still, however, pack gourmet.

I don't think I'll ever love baseball the way I love the theater, but things about it make it more exciting sometimes. For one thing, there's no rehearsal in baseball. Practice isn't the same as rehearsal. Rehearsal means you get the lines and the moves down pat. Practice means you prepare for anything that can happen and probably will. If you have an off night in the theater you get depressed. If you have an off night in baseball you lose. And my family can see a baseball game and eat for under a thousand dollars.

There are things about the business of baseball that nauseate and confuse me. I choose not to understand concepts like free agency and salary caps, and I don't understand why people can't be content with million-dollar salaries when that kind of pay would make me feel like a million bucks. No one has been able to explain to me why, a few weeks after winning the World Series, a series I did not miss thirty seconds of, half the Yankees were traded and now I'll have to learn a whole new line-up next season. I bought into all the hype about how those guys really loved each other and worked as a team. So why are they splitting up? I'm not broken up about it, just curious. And it doesn't matter. None of the pettiness for me interferes with the romance of the game itself. As long as Joe loves Marilyn, baseball will still be romantic.

My boys taught me something about throwing and catching that they knew instinctively. It feels good. Something about how I throw the ball and you catch it and you throw it and I catch it connects us. Ions pass back and forth between people without the people themselves ever having to touch each other. It's a non-threatening way of bonding that requires equal amounts of effort and trust from both players. I'm not yet well versed enough to expound on the baseball-as-life metaphor, but I can see how baseball enriches life and how much of life is in baseball. No cowards allowed. One can't be shy on the ballfield. Body language counts. You can't avert your eyes when a ball is coming at you. Face-to-face playing is compulsory. My sons can't stay angry at each other when they play ball. It's silent, interpersonal communication that demands synchronicity, and it's completely different from dressing and undressing dolls. I know. I've done both. I wish all girls would.

I Menstruate. They Don't.

Today was just another day in the fourth grade. Chris Sanderson was punished for selling photographic excerpts from his sister's diary to all his friends who have siblings her age. Ryan Schwartz won the science contest for eating bugs and not dying. And my son Andrew informed his class that I had my period. Peter Pataski practically puked up his peanut butter and marshmallow sandwich because it was so disgusting—not the sandwich, my period.

Andrew doesn't usually do things that could get him into trouble with the authorities. I think he was perplexed that some of the kids hadn't learned all about menstruation from their mothers. He expected the uneducated to be grateful to him for taking time out from lunch to demonstrate the physiological details by spooning his Campbell's Tomato Soup into a napkin as a visual aid.

I'll be getting calls tonight. Six or seven mothers will phone to say, "My son (or daughter) heard the most amusing biology lecture from your son today, and I thought I'd call just to make you aware of the information your child is disseminating to his peers because I'm sure he didn't hear it from you." There will be a long pause while each of these mothers silently adds, "you liberal, pro-choice, gay sympathizing, anti-family values, feminist democrat!" I will promise to get to the bottom of it, hang up, and finish the fat-free hot fudge, chocolate chip, peanut butter cup brownie ice cream (whoops, yogurt) sundae that my doctor prescribed for cramping.

I don't mind that the boys know about my period. I'm glad my liberal, pro-choice, gay sympathizing, anti-family values, feminist democrat husband explained it to them. After all, unjustifiable but ingenious and torturous forms of mental and physical punishment, sporadic periods of acute dementia, and complete and heartless withdrawal of affection are monthly facts of life in our house. Maybe knowledge will do for my sons what evening primrose oil, vitamin B6, vitamin E, diuretics, exercise, and meditation couldn't do for me. Maybe it will help them cope. Or maybe knowledge is power and they'll murder me in my sleep following a premenstrual conniption. That would be okay too.

What I do mind is being asked if I have my period because I put cauliflower, which they know I know they hate, on the dinner table. I really, really mind that. And I mind being accused of menstruation *every* time I tell them they look like slobs. They *do* look like slobs. Far more often than I menstruate. I also really mind that I can't unconsciously slip a wayward Cocoa Puff into my mouth without hearing, "Chocolate! Sleep at a friend's tonight!"

I really really mind that my sons will never know what it feels like to pass a two-liter blood clot with each grocery bag you lift. They won't know the joy of lying on the family room floor with your bouncing baby boy and having him bounce on your uterus, sending your tampon flying into the TV. I also mind that they won't ever be stuck in a car behind a farm vehicle on a lonesome, romantic rural road when the automatic drip activates and the nearest drugstore is fifty miles away and closed. I can't help it, but I mind that.

I want my boys to know the truth about menstruation. But what is the truth? I want them to believe that menstruating women can perform as well as most men in most situations. I want them to believe that our periods don't slow us down, string us out, screw us up, or do us in. And I know they don't believe this when they see me slowed down, strung out, screwed up, and done in. Therein lies the dilemma.

I can either cope stoically and silently with an ever worsening variety of symptoms and syndromes, giving them the false impression that menstruating is a piece of cake that requires no accommodation, or I can let them be privy to my agony in the hope of moving them to noble acts of compassion such as getting their own juice. If I do that however, I am an accomplice in fostering the stereotype of the whining, helpless woman. I want to teach my sons about empathy. I hope it is not true that you have to experience misfortune yourself in order to be fully sympathetic to it. Most people who help the blind cross the street are not blind themselves. But do I want to liken menstruation to a disability? I think not. It's all too confusing.

How will my sons learn to be understanding if understanding is never required of them? Right or wrong, I choose not to be Supermom. I can't be Supermom because I *have* no choice in this matter. When the hormones rush and my brain becomes as bloated as my stomach, it becomes physically and emotionally impossible for me to give a damn about what kind of messages I'm sending to my sons. It takes all the strength I can summon just to inquire about their day. Forget about listening to the answer. I have let them know that menstruating may be a piece of cake for some women, but it isn't for me. Only a piece of cake is, and it better be chocolate and I want it *now*!

Gloria Steinam wrote a classic essay about what would happen if men menstruated. She postulated that they would build an altar to the God of Menstruation (the God, of course, being a man). The global workplace would initiate flextime to accommodate the monthly incapacitation of men of menstruating age. They'd hold festivals to celebrate it and contests to see who could do it longest, hardest, reddest. I think she may be right. On the other hand, they might just kill themselves.

Me Want Car

Dan was far too exhausted from soccer practice to take the late bus home today. What if he were to fall asleep on the ride and miss his stop? He heard that some kid did that once and almost spent the weekend in the bus garage. Cleverly reasoning that if I wasn't home, I wouldn't have to take calls from the irate mothers of Andrew's classmates over the menstruation debacle, I agreed to retrieve him from school.

I had memorized my instructions. I was to pull around to the back of the building instead of picking him up in the convenient circular driveway at the entrance, where the rest of the kids with Friday afternoon bus anxiety wait for their parents who have cool cars. According to Dan, my car is totally uncool and getting a lift home in it is for him only a slightly less mortifying ordeal than waking up in a dark, deserted bus garage. He's right. My car is uncool, but who cares, I ask. It gets him where he has to go.

Apparently, there is a new car on the market called the Testerosa. This is the car he hungers for. One need not be a linguist to recognize that this vehicle can only be named after the male hormone. It's probably setting new sales records. As far as I know there is not yet a car on the road called the Estrogina. I doubt that the Estrogina is so much as a twinkle in any car designer's eye. The fact that the male genitalia resembles a gear shift may have something to do with that gender's obsession with motor vehicles. Maybe there is something erotic about playing with a gear shift. Boys seem to enjoy playing with cars almost as much as they enjoy playing with themselves. But this is speculation. It could just be that boys think cars are cool.

My mother began working full time outside the home when I was a senior in high school, which gave me exclusive use of the car between eight-thirty and five. Her car was a huge red station wagon with wood on the side. It didn't occur to me that huge red station wagons with wood on the side were totally uncool. The car got me to and from school faster than I could walk and that was cool enough for me.

My first bought-and-paid-for car was a Ford Pinto. I purchased it when I was twenty-two. The gas tanks used to explode on Ford Pintos. It didn't occur to me that this was totally uncool. The car was what I could afford and it was all mine and that was cool enough for me.

Dan is three years away from driving, but he knows he wants a Testerosa. Or a Jeep convertible. Or a Corvette. Used would be okay. New would be better. Why do I have to talk about this now?

And how did he know that the sound my car makes when I start it indicates that my fan belt is broken? When has he ever seen a fan belt, broken or otherwise? And how come he can't recognize the states by their shapes even after putting the puzzle map together, but he recognizes the shape of every car on the road and we never even take him to car lots?

How do boys make those car noises with their lips? I can't get mine to vibrate that quickly. And why do even really big boys like really small cars?

If Dan insists we talk about cars three years before he can legally drive, I feel it's okay to start scaring him with gruesome stories of accidents. I tell him every grizzly accident story I can remember. My friend Elayne's precious son suffered a complete and permanent loss of short-term memory because of a car accident he didn't cause. Elayne, who still can laugh and enjoy life, is my hero and would be even if all she managed to do in a day is get up in the morning. My friend Susan's daughter was sideswiped by a truck and will never play field hockey again. She was the team captain. The woman who sits next to me at the manicurist pays half price because she lost one arm in an accident last month. I'm not groping for humor here; this is true. I am the Dow Jones of accident statistics and I have successfully used them to scare myself silly. They've had no effect on Dan.

He does listen to my ravings, however, so in return I spent an hour with him last week calculating how many lawns he would have to mow over the next three years to be able to afford a Corvette. A Jeep. A used Chevy. I have no idea what the dreaded Testerosa costs. He told me that he has lowered his expectations considerably. I told him it would be wise to surrender all expectations because he will not be getting a car when he is sixteen regardless of whether or not he can afford one. He doesn't believe me. He thinks that not having wheels will make him totally uncool and I would never allow that to happen to him.

He's wrong. I haven't even decided whether or not I'll allow him to get his license when he's sixteen. The trouble is, he can't go anywhere without a car. At the risk of sounding as old as I am, I admit that when I was young, we had public transportation. Even in some suburbs. We had sidewalks and sometimes even used them for getting from place to place. Of course there weren't all that many places that you wanted to get to, but I could walk to my grandmother's house or to the shopping center or the ice cream parlour. I'm not sure my sons know that their legs can be used for transportation. So they dream about owning cars. Girls dream about owning boys who own cars.

It is my job and my right to worry. I take my worrying seriously and I've become proficient. The trouble with worrying so far in advance, though, is that I'm wasting valuable mental energy I could be using to write the Anna Karenina exercise book, *Abs Under Steel*, or solve our national health care crisis. How does a mother instill in her sons a healthy fear of body mutilation without scaring them or herself to death?

I don't know, but I know I'm going to come between Dan and his dream car. When I decide to let him drive, he'll have to borrow my ugly but safe suburban tank and hide it behind buildings, and that's cool enough for me.

Does That Grunt Mean Hello?

A chapter about greetings and salutations would appropriately belong at the beginning of a book. However, situating it just past its rightful place illustrates the fact that despite years of salutation instruction, my boys still don't seem to understand how or when to say hello. Dan and Andrew will end a conversation in the middle and pick it up three days later just where they left off, expecting us to follow their train of thought as if it had just left the station. Visitors tell us they feel instantly at home in our home. I don't think it's because of our warm hospitality. Rather, it's because the boys don't acknowledge that anyone has ever arrived, left the premises, or returned. It's as if our guests are a constant metaphysical presence here.

I don't understand why all the boys I've ever known are salutation-challenged, because greetings are among the easiest things we ever have to learn. They can be learned by rote. They require no abstract reasoning skills. If comprehension proves difficult for a child, salutations can be mimicked without anyone being the wiser. Oral language isn't mandatory. A wink, a wave, a nod are all widely accepted as friendly greetings, not to mention a simple smile. Generally, a child's first smile is the best sign of salutation readiness. "Smile at Grandma" is a universal first salutation command.

Many parents believe that a properly executed salutation is the single best indicator that a child has received proper civility training. If a child achieves a high civility rating as evidenced by the finesse of his greetings, the score on the parents' proficiency scale will be likewise impressive.

We all want at least the outward appearance of competence as parents. In many situations our children act as our advance team. We rely upon them heavily for PR purposes. So we start pounding acceptable salutations into their little heads early on. "How do you do?" "It's nice to meet you." "It's good to see you again." A small, but venerable lexicon. Easy to teach. A snap to learn. So why do my boys insist upon ignoring people entirely or greeting them with a "Yo," a grunt I don't know how to spell, or a physical assault?

Last Friday, upon arriving home from school, Dan had to contend with greeting me, his two brothers, and his grandmother. I was greeted with a snack request. His grandmother was simply ignored. Andrew was greeted with a karate chop to the shoulder, and Zack was hurled at least five yards from the kitchen entrance onto the den sofa. Grandma was the only one of us who demanded an upgraded salutation. She managed to finagle a hug. Okay, so this is no big deal. We're

just family. I don't greet my husband at the end of every business day with "Hello. It's nice to see you again." A simple
"Hi, honey" seems to do. On dull days he gets a "Hi." Yesterday, he got a harangue. But out in the world I can and do
greet people courteously. I'm not sure my sons have made
the distinction between family people and out-in-the-world
people.

I went with my husband on a business trip to Chicago
one day last winter. A dear friend and former college room-
mate lives there, and I was delighted to reconnect with her for
a day. Sylvia is the mother of three daughters. She and I were
chatting in the living room when the girls arrived home from
school. I was struck dumb by the greetings I received. The
girls came in through the front door (notice the use of the
word "came," rather than bounded or fell or bulldozed their
way through) and Sylvia said, "Girls, this is my oldest and
most special friend, Karin." In perfect Von Trapp style, each
girl approached me and shook my hand.

"Hi. I'm Emily."

"Nice to meet you. I'm Tina."

"My mother told us all about you. I'm Julia."

It would have been terrifying if it hadn't been such a pleasure. Now, I know Sylvia. She's a tad more formal than I am,
but she's no Christopher Plummer. There were no whistles
blown, no military marching required—just a polite greeting.
Oh God, she not only had perfect hair, but perfect children as
well. I know all about salutation mind games. I knew these

kids had been drilled to make Sylvia look like Harriet Nelson. And I fell into the trap anyway. I liked them. Instantly. It was the politesse. I awarded Sylvia many points for parental proficiency and decided I would never let her meet my children. I hated them. After all, they had been coached too. I had been a salutation drill sergeant. And I have yet to see them greet anyone as I had been greeted here.

A few weeks later, an important client of my husband's came to drop off some papers at our house. He was standing in the doorway, about to leave, when Dan and Andrew decided to play basketball. They raced toward the door only to find it barred by this rather portly man.

"This is Mr. Burrows," I said. "He works with Dad."

Each of them muttered a single, unintelligible syllable as they attacked the challenge of manipulating their bodies around this bovine figure. Rather than politely asking him to move, or better yet, using a different egress, they executed impressive feats of contortion to slip out around him, barely escaping the embarrassment (mine, not theirs) of knocking him in his three-piece suit onto our red gravel driveway. As he drove away, I'm sure he was wondering in which jungle these children had been raised. I'm sure he thought I was suffering an embarrassment beyond the power of therapy to cure. He was wrong. I don't hold on to salutation embarrassment. By the time his car reached the bottom of our driveway, I had already moved on to gratitude that the big boys had decided against using Zack as their basketball that evening.

Now let's talk phone. I don't expect to get my phone messages and never do, but mothers of daughters don't expect to get their phone messages either. However, I could live without comments from friends such as "I called you yesterday. I think a dog answered." Callers have a better chance of comprehending the tongue clicking of a Kung Bushman on the telephone than of interpreting Dan's grunts and snorts. It is remarkable how he can answer any question with one syllable.

"How are you?"

"Fine."

"Is your mom home?"

"No."

"You just won the Publisher's Clearinghouse contest."

"Great."

"We have your prize money in the van, but we got lost on the way to your house. Can you give us directions from route 413?"

"Szxft."

I've told him that vocabulary is not a precious resource we're in danger of depleting. He should feel free to employ as many words as he likes. He answered me in one not nice syllable.

To his credit, Andrew is polite and ingratiating on the telephone. But forgets to let me know that I'm wanted. He will nicely say "Just a moment" and put the receiver down and forget all about it. Callers are left dangling indefinitely in telephone purgatory.

I do not believe salutation ineptitude suggests overall etiquette incompetence. I'm typically proud of the way my children handle themselves in situations requiring a high degree of social savvy. In fact, I am often complimented on their manners. Boys are simply salutation-challenged—a condition that I theorize is neurologically based and linked to their general inability to see what is two feet in front of them. First you have to know a person is *there* before you can realize a necessity to acknowledge that person's presence.

Or perhaps the rest of us are hypocrites. More often than not, we ask "How are you?" when we couldn't care less about the answer. We say "Have a nice day" to people we wish would get hit by a bus. Women are especially conditioned to be polite even when common sense tells us that the person we're being polite to is slime. We say "Nice to see you" to the guy from the IRS. We apologize to waitresses when we send back dinners that have arrived burnt or raw. We give Christmas gifts to our manicurists and hairdressers, even though we've been paying them weekly or monthly and they should be giving us presents. We do things out of a graciousness that is not compulsory in men. Could it be that my boys have it right? Does a simple "Hi" suffice in most situations? Maybe. If it's intelligible.

Letting Hoppy Go

We visited Hoppy today and now I have to take back everything I said about salutation ineptitude. It is only homo sapiens that boys don't know how to greet politely. Canines, felines, reptiles, and amphibians are received like royalty. I knew when I started popping boys that a pet or a series of pets was in my future. This was not a happy thought. I am not a pet person. Dogs and cats give me asthma. I find it disgusting that fish live in their own toilets. Birds are obnoxious in the middle of the night. I considered getting a chimpanzee once because they look cute in overalls and Keds, but their table manners are atrocious.

Whenever my sons take up their "We need a pet" campaign, I gently remind them that we live in the country. We live in harmony with all of God's creatures and I'm certain that Bambi's descendants, with whom we happily coexist, would be honored for us to think of them as our pets. It doesn't fly. Pets, they tell me, are only pets if they can pee on your carpet, everybody except us has a pet, and would I for once leave God and Disney out of something. I was sympathetic. After all, I was weaned on Lassie and Flipper and Rin-Tin-Tin and Flicka. Every book that has a boy in it has a dog or a cat or a cow in it, too. Try to think of one that doesn't. Okay, Mike Mulligan had a steam shovel, but she barked like a dog and was just as dirty. I would never be able to live with myself if I caused psychological damage by disregarding their heart-felt pleas for a pet. Also, I was already denying Dan a car, and I figured a pet would be a nice consolation prize. So I caved.

Having rationalized myself to near-death, I let them bring Hoppy the frog into my life. Here was an opportunity for my sons to learn how to nurture something, to put someone else's needs before their own, to see what it takes to be a respon-sible caretaker. I thought raising a frog would give them a tiny glimpse into the glamorous world of parenting. I would have bet that amphibians never say thank you when you feed them, and I liked that. Perhaps this experience would teach them empathy. For their little charge of course, but particularly for me. I began to view this frog thing as my obligation as a mother of sons and a feminist. Never would I say no to boys who wanted desperately to succor a small living thing. Especially if that living thing could be kept away from the carpet. So, after I suggested that "Hoppy" might not be the most creative name for a frog living in a writer's home, Hoppy came to live with us.

Andrew had captured Hoppy in the drainage basin we like to think of as a pond. I didn't think it was fair of him to remove the little guy from all that was familiar to him, including probably his own mother, but I kept God and Disney out of it for once.

With the possible exception of Kermit, no frog has ever been so adored. The boys, whose legs, you recall, have never been used to get places fast except on a ballfield, sprinted up our driveway every day at breakneck speed to shower Hoppy with the kind of salutations I am personally reserving for the arrival of the Messiah. I would gladly have grown warts if I thought it would precipitate daily reunions such as those. Instead, I willed myself, as I had with baseball, to get positive and get involved. And I did.

Here are all the lessons I have learned about frogs:

1. There is no such thing as packaged frog food. Frogs won't eat fish food or bird food. Frogs eat bugs. Crickets are the bugs of choice.

2. The crickets you feed the frog must be alive. Frogs won't eat crickets they don't catch themselves. I began to have trouble with this frog thing during lesson #2.

3. You can buy live crickets at most pet stores. They will put them in a plastic bag for you. Twelve crickets will last about a week.

4. One cricket-size plastic bag contains only enough air for forty minutes. I learned this the first time all the crickets died waiting for the boys to get home from school to feed Hoppy. You will have to feed the crickets to the frog yourself if your children are in school when you stop at the pet store.

My children are in school every day and participate in after-school sports on most days. Consequently, they are free only when the pet store is closed. I became the sole frog feeder and began to have even more trouble with this frog thing.

5. Don't forget what you learned in lesson #2. Crickets have to stay alive. That means they have to breathe and eat. You have to put a piece of potato in the crickets' environment. It's called a food chain. Fourth grade science. Food chain. Fortunately, crickets, unlike children, are happy to eat their potato without butter or milk.

6. Crickets drown in water. I learned this the first time all the crickets drowned when I put them in the tank with the frog, who must have water in order to live. As you already know, frogs won't eat dead crickets, so you have to make sure there is plenty of dry land in your aquarium.

7. If you put too many crickets in the aquarium with the frog at one time, the frog will have a nervous breakdown. I learned this from the pet store guy when I told him that Hoppy was catatonic. Apparently, crickets like to sit on frogs' heads and eyes. Frogs have no way of brushing the crickets away. Wouldn't this make you crazy? Here's the solution. Make a separate environment for the crickets and the potato, and put it where the frog can't see it. Chimpanzees with bad table manners began to look good to me. Feed the frog no more than two crickets a day.

8. Once frogs have nervous breakdowns, they never recover.

9. Frogs, even catatonic frogs with unoriginal names, are very happy when you return them to the drainage basin they call home. Boys are not.

Hoppy was clearly not thriving in our home. I was pretty sure early on that he was miserable, but I held my tongue. I didn't want to force my children into a decision and later suffer their resentment. I was willing to ignore the frog's feelings. I was willing to sacrifice his very life in order for my children to grow from this experience. Mothers do that. Fortunately, my children came to a humanitarian decision on their own before we had to stage a frog funeral. With great empathy and ceremony they let Hoppy, their fast amphibian friend, go. And he went. Fast.

One more thing I learned about frogs is this. They're not like babies. Not even a little bit. They're not even like cats or dogs. Frogs never let you know that they like you. They don't smile or coo or lick your face or wag a tail. My boys held Hoppy and stroked him and said nice things to him and made sure his tank was somewhat less than totally, disgustingly filthy, and the whole time he lived with us, Hoppy held his emotions in check. It takes a warm heart and strength of character to steadfastly love something that doesn't love you back. And they did it. He was an ungrateful pain in the neck and they loved him and still do and visit him often. We know that the frogs they pull out of the drainage basin pond are probably not Hoppy, but we don't speak of this.

My sons' caretaking techniques need work. But learning

how to change a diaper or mix up the oatmeal isn't the vital part of parenthood. The vital part they've aced.

Belching, Farting, and Other Table Manners

Hoppy never managed to leap his way into my heart, but he had some admirable qualities. His table manners were impeccable. He never once spit out his crickets, and no matter how large the cricket he ingested, as far as I could tell, he never belched. The same cannot be said of my sons.

It would be too easy and unoriginal to use the "feeding time at the zoo" analogy in regard to dining with my brood. Besides, my children don't eat like monkeys. Monkeys can hold food with their toes. My children are required to wear shoes at the table.

To be honest, I've seen girls with horrendous table manners. I've seen pigtails dance in spaghetti sauce. Dinner doesn't get much more disgusting than that. Dan has a friend who is a girl who can fit an entire slice of pizza into her mouth at once, just as he can. It would be unfair to my children to attribute their uncouth behavior to the simple fact that they are boys.

The difference between dining with daughters and dining with sons, I've decided, has less to do with *how* they eat or *what* they eat (If it doesn't look, smell, or taste like pizza, forget it) than with what they do *while* they eat. Boys stand. Sometimes they straddle the chair. I've seen Andrew complete a meal while touching his chair with every one of his body parts except his rear end. The body part for which chairs were invented never made contact. My boys play mini basketball with brussels sprouts. They set up competitions: who can refrain from laughing the longest with a mouthful of applesauce, who can balance a glass on a mountain of salt. And of course, their favorite: who can belch the loudest. This is what separates the girls from the boys. I have yet to see girls engage in belching competitions. And believe me, I look.

Obviously this book is a catharsis for me, so it would be pointless to lie and say that I have never belched. I have, even as an adult. I have also picked my nose, passed gas, and once or twice, while experiencing acute cold symptoms, chewed my food with my mouth open.

The human body has ways of insuring that its needs are met. I am, as are the rest of us, sometimes called upon to attend to my body's most primitive needs. Obediently, I do whatever it takes to achieve homeostasis. But I don't make a religion out of it.

Belching is to my sons what gospel music is to the rest of us. The longer, the louder, the fuller you can make the sound, the closer you stand to God. And if you do it in the belcher's house of worship, a restaurant, it counts as a hymn.

In certain cultures, belching is considered a physical way of demonstrating that you love the cooking. I am not a member of any of these cultures. In my culture, belching is a physical way of demonstrating that you hate the cook. Or at least don't respect her enough to avoid offending her sensibilities.

It has been pointed out to me that sometimes you just can't help it. Okay, I can buy that. But what about standing up, announcing that you are going to do it, widening your mouth to the size of an open garage, cupping your hands into megaphone position, rolling your eyes, doing it, doing it again, sighing with relief that you've done it, and then convulsing into peals of laughter for twenty minutes? That I think you can help.

I explain ways of squelching a belch. It takes stomach control, will-power, and practice. "Wouldn't it be easier for you to cover your ears?" they reply. "That doesn't require any practice at all!" Oh goody—sarcasm. The beauty of a belch is definitely enhanced by sarcasm. I leave the table. They accuse me of being humorless. I tell them to show me some humor and we'll see if they're right. But enough about belching. On to farting.

My husband earned a Ph.D. I say this not to brag but to illustrate that there is no correlation between the level of your education and the sophistication of your humor. Harold doesn't think a joke is funny unless there's a fart in it somewhere. That's not entirely true. Jokes or anecdotes can be funny sans bathroom references, but the addition of flatulence elevates them to levels worthy of hysteria. Why is this? My boys understand that while I will merely excoriate them for belching in public, the consequences for purposeful farting are far more dire. They have managed to absorb some baseline etiquette over the years, and it's been quite some time since they've humiliated me by breaking wind in public. They remain, however, an appreciative audience for any unfortunate person who executes the unspeakable within earshot. On these occasions I wish I had closed the womb after Dan emerged. An only child will usually extinguish a behavior that isn't reinforced. But a child whose laughter or mimicry or noisemaking is greeted with delight by his siblings will redouble his efforts in order to keep the reinforcement coming. Count on it. So now you have a prepubescent maniac laughing until snot runs out of his nose. He chokes on every inhalation. He holds his stomach. He snorts. He looks like he's having one hell of a good time. And that is frankly, totally unfair to little brother. Let the rivalry begin. Big brother can laugh louder than little brother. Just listen. Littlest brother can snort better than either of the big ones. Just listen. Middle brother can simulate fart noises with his hand and his armpit. But not as loudly as big brother can. And all the brothers are excellent finger pointers. The poor creature who has the audacity or bad luck to fart in front of my children can kiss his anonymity good-bye. My heart breaks for this pathetic object of ridicule.

All mothers like to hear their children laugh. In this

pursuit, I lost my head one day and rented "Blazing Saddles." (Okay, it's rated R, which makes me a terrible mother, but compared to today's R-rated movies it was tame, so maybe I'm merely bad.) I thought I would have to administer CPR to Andrew during the campfire scene. My coolness rating rose ten points that day. But I didn't do myself any favors, because now they can't look at a bean without being gross.

I realized sometime last year that my reactions to belching and farting have conformed to all the stages of mourning that Elizabeth Kübler-Ross describes in her book, *On Death and Dying*. The first stage is denial. Does there exist a mother who has never denied that the crass monkeys she happens to be with are her children? Stage two is anger. Uh-huh. Stage three is bargaining. Child psychologists like to call this a reward-punishment parenting maneuver. I think when you pay your children to act human, it's more like bargaining. Stage four is acceptance. Acceptance is the hardest part. It's the part where you tell yourself over and over that they'll grow out of it—that chances are they will respect their future girlfriends more than they do you and in the name of love will suppress their baser instincts—that you can't judge a person by his manners. Richard Speck looked like he never belched once in his life and how would you like to be *his* mother? Little by little I have accepted the fact that their sensibilities differ from my own. I don't get apoplectic when I sit on the whoopee cushion or homicidal at the sight of a half-chewed hot dog in someone's mouth. It comes with the territory. Which is why I've staked out my own.

It is a six-foot-long cast-iron clawfoot tub and it is my most favorite possession. If I put potpourri in a basket and bath oils in the tub and candles on the shelf and if I play Streisand really loud, I can almost tune out the nightly belch marathon one floor below me.

Boys' Noise

Tuning out the non-belching related noise is far more challenging. They'd have to stamp Sun•Maid on my forehead if I retreated to my tub to escape noise entirely. I'd be a raisin by now for sure from all that soaking. Instead, I keep this quote by the wonderful writer and philosopher Colette right above my desk and I use it for my mantra. She wrote:

"Repose of mind and body is not dependent on silence."

Well, thank God. If I depended on silence for my personal serenity, I would have long ago had to go to my grave to find it. We who spawn multiple boys invite constant clamor into our world. If the activities our offspring engage in aren't inherently noisy, boys will overcompensate by whooping, hollering, and bellowing twice as loudly as they would if they were playing with, let's say, a jackhammer. One can't play race car without sound effects. Or bulldozer. Or cops and robbers. Or sports of any kind. House, on the other hand, can be played in hushed tones. "Shh, the baby is sleeping" is a vital element in the game of house. Tea parties require elegant

Jane Austenesque repartee. "Let's throw your little brother down the well," on the other hand, evokes a certain amount of screaming—usually from little brother.

Air-conditioning bills for boy-only families are exorbitant. For years I was embarrassed to open my windows in the spring or summer for fear that the neighbors would call the police. It always sounds as if somebody is getting killed in here.

Come to think of it, this would be an ideal place to commit murder because the people in charge here have a firm nonresponse policy when it comes to screaming or threatening. Harold and I used to respond to cries for help until they became so frequent that we could never finish anything we started—not a meal, not a phone conversation, not a television show—not even the activity that propelled us into this child-infested environment in the first place. We were interrupted so often for unnecessary interventions that we decided to ignore all bloodless altercations. Only blood will get us off our rear ends now, and sure enough, the house has been somewhat more quiet since this practice was instituted. The boys still scream like banshees, but we have stopped reacting by screaming back at them, so at least we don't have to listen to our own noise anymore.

Occasionally, when we fear that someone might get maimed or killed, whether it be during a genuine fight or playful battering, we demand that they separate and play quietly by themselves for an hour or two. In my dreams they spend this time reading. In real life they play with either the Nintendo or the computer, both of which emit repetitive pseudo-musical tunes that drive you slowly toward psychosis by staying inside your head for weeks at a time. Uncharacteristic of myself as it is, when it comes to electronic games I prefer the violent ones. The intermittent sound of empires blowing up doesn't create half the migraine that the unrelenting doo-doo-de-doos of, let's say, Super Mario Brothers, cause. I've tried to get the boys to turn the sound off when they play. Dan says anyone who went to as many Who concerts as I did should know that volume is half the fun. I counter that in their whole lives The Who never played doo-doo-de-doo.

Several months ago we bought an intercom. We logically figured that while it would have no effect on the cacophony of sounds emanating from within a single room in the house, it would at least relieve us from some of the inter-room racket. HAH! Now we hear this.

Andrew: (calling from the bedroom to the basement) DAAAAAAAN! (No response. Pause. Second attempt.) DAAAAAAAN!

Dan: WHAAAAAAAAAAAAT?

Andrew: (screaming) I HAVE TO ASK YOU SOMETHING!

Dan: (screaming back) USE THE INTERCOM!!!!

Andrew: (screaming) WHAAAAAAAAAAT?

Dan: (screaming at a volume approaching sonic boom) USE THE INTERCOM!!!!

Andrew: (screaming into the intercom) DAAAAAAN!

Dan: (screaming into the intercom) YOU MORON! DO YOU WANT TO KILL ME? YOU DON'T HAVE TO SCREAM LIKE THIS INTO THE INTERCOM!!!

Listening to a conversation such as this is probably what killed Henry Higgins.

It is most likely too late for Harold and me to regain the hearing we've lost as a result of parenting three boys. It's an occupational hazard like black lung disease. And speaking of lungs, Dan's are now bigger and stronger than mine. Never having been a mouse, I used to raise my voice at him to express my anger or disapproval. At some point—I think when he became thirteen—he raised his voice back at me. I was surprised but not intimidated. A few days ago, however, I yelled at him over something that I can no longer remember and that obviously isn't all that important. He yelled back. Louder than I had yelled at him. I raised my volume. He did the same. Back and forth we went until I thought my spleen would explode and come out my mouth. I was hoarse and dizzy and red and swooning from the exertion. He could have raised the intensity even more had it been necessary. Harold stared in disbelief. Finally, there was nothing to do but laugh. I looked and felt like the village idiot, drooling and scratching my head and wondering what it was I had just been through. When I regained equilibrium, I realized that I had been through the inevitable. I would have to find a new way of making a point.

It was shattering to realize that I was contributing to the noise factor in my home. I could claim that I had to scream to be noticed, but I think if I had tried, I could have found other ways of getting their attention. Anyway, I am delighted to admit that this epiphany has lowered the household din. Also, Dan has a social life now, so he's not home as often.

I opened the windows yesterday. I needed some fresh air. Little Laurie, three acres away, screamed at her sister. Even during a decade of soccer games and wrestling matches and Jean-Claude Van Damme movies—even during all of those Who concerts, I've never heard anything like it. It wasn't how loud it was that made me squirm; it was how high it was. The frequency of that scream made my teeth hurt. It was the worst sound I had ever heard. Until Little Laurie's sister screamed back. The frequency of *that* scream should have sent the neighborhood dogs running for cover. It is gruesome to imagine living in a house with children who can scream like that. I asked my friend Edye if her daughter was capable of such screeching.

"About four times a week," was the answer.

I'll choose volume over pitch every time. I'll take a hundred boys screaming their heads off about nothing, over one Little Laurie screeching for a legitimate reason. And after rereading *Gigi*, by Colette, I'm changing my mantra. No wonder she could have repose of body and soul. Not once did her little protagonist scream.

Advice and Sex

It was back to the advice manuals for me when the time came to have a serious talk with my sons about sex. I had stopped reading how-to books when Dan was nine. From the day my pregnancy dipstick turned blue until Dan's ninth birthday, I devoured every book, magazine, pamphlet, or bumper sticker I could find that used the word parent as a verb. It is what baby boomers do to try to get things right. Here is the result of my synthesis of the state-of-the-art parenting techniques espoused by the greatest parenting minds of the early Eighties.

One: The greatest parenting minds of the early Eighties disagree with each other on nearly everything to do with child rearing except for consistency. Consistency is the fundamental principle of effective parenting.

Two: The child psychologists who write the advice books never tell you that consistency is virtually impossible to achieve, particularly for former hippies who love life precisely because of its capriciousness. Consistency for me requires a Herculean effort that I am not up to.

Three: The experts also fail to report on the results of their own parenting experiences. They interview thousands, maybe millions, of parents like me for their statistics and anecdotes, but I don't want to know how other parents like me fare with their children. I want to know how the greatest parenting minds of our time are doing. Forget it. It's classified information. All I know is that I recently became friendly with a local child psychologist and her child is wack-o, so there you go.

I stopped reading the advice, held my breath, and tried to parent my sons intuitively and as consistently as could reasonably be expected, while at the same time trying to catch up on the best sellers I had missed over the past nine years. I'm sure I wasn't perfect, but I did love them consistently, which goes a long way toward compensating for minor errors in judgment. When it came time to talk about sex though, it was back to the bookstore for me. I really, really wanted to get this right. Not the physiology and mechanics part. That was Harold's job and it had already been attended to in small increments since Dan was three. I put myself in charge of teaching the boys about the non-physical elements. About love and respect. Harold had attended to this too, I'm sure, but as a woman, a mother, a subscriber to *Ms.*, and a supporter of Anita Hill, raising sons who are loving and respectful is not a personal challenge, but a personal imperative. I had to speak my piece.

I have a friend whose son threw a party last year that became a spin-the-bottle fest. When she went downstairs ostensibly to refill the potato chip bowls, she discovered one of the girls huddling in the corner. This rather shy and beautiful child had refused to kiss the boy who had spun the Coke bottle in her direction. He was visibly hostile as he hovered over her menacingly.

"You have to kiss me," he bellowed. "The rules are the rules."

My girlfriend's mothering skills are the envy of every woman in the PTO. She has a twelve-year-old daughter, which makes her a thirteen-year-old-boy's nightmare because she interferes. She interfered that night. Bigtime. She took this frightened lamb by the hand and stroked her hair and assured her that she didn't ever have to kiss anyone she didn't want to kiss—that she was not a bad sport or a tease or any of the other unfair adolescent labels her partymates were tossing at her. This boy, my friend explained, was out of line, and if he did so much as look cross-eyed at any of the girls in that room again, he would be banished from the house. Well, there went everyone's good time, and after hearing the story, there went I into my sons' rooms, armed with advice and ready to chat.

When I began to write this book, Dan still decorated his bedroom walls with NBA posters rather than photo enlargements of the *Sports Illustrated* Swimsuit Model of the Year contestants. He chose to have an all-male football and pizza party for his Bar Mitzvah, rather than the more traditional boy-girl dinner dance or sock hop. As far as I knew, he had yet to kiss a girl or even talk to one. (All that has changed now as this book becomes a reality, but let's talk about "then.")

Andrew has hoarded my Victoria's Secret catalogues since he turned six. I don't search his room, but when we packed up to move, about two hundred of them fell out from behind the tiny door in his closet that leads to the crawl space. Since the articles in the Victoria's Secret catalogue are of the underwear rather than the literary variety, I assumed that he liked the pictures. By nine years old he had asked me to explain how French kissing works. He also wanted to know how you decide upon whom you are going to marry, whether or not you get to choose your own partner at ninth grade make-out parties, and whether they serve chips at those events or if eating is not allowed. An individualized approach to the sex talk was clearly necessary.

I approached Dan about a week after Harold had finally finished explaining sex to him, which was about a year after the school had explained it and three years after his friends had explained it.

"Are there any questions you would like to ask me because I'm a woman and might be able to help explain a teenage girl's behavior or sensibility?"

I wasn't going to be taken by surprise. I had prepared wise, thoughtful answers to anything he could have thrown at me.

"Nope," he said. "I'm going to go shoot some hoops."

I was taken by surprise. I hadn't prepared for a brush-off. He's my son! We're supposed to share!

"Are you sure, honey? You don't have to be embarrassed with me. I'm your mother."

"That's exactly why this is embarrassing." He blushed. This was not going according to the how-tos.

"Do you know that getting flowers can turn a woman on?"

"Mooooooooooooom!"

"It's true. Romantic gestures like giving flowers or complimenting her on her looks or on how smart she is (especially how smart she is) or offering to help with a chore or project or simply being interested in what she has to say are all just as important to a woman as the sex act itself?"

"I knooooooooooooooooooooow!"

"How do you know? What women do you talk to? I want names."

"You tell me just about every minute."

"So you understand why that boy was out of line at Susie's party, and why Susie's mother got so angry?"

"YEEEEEEEEEEESSSS! LEAVE ME ALONE ALREADY!"

He was right. I don't let up. Every time Harold brings me flowers or pays me a compliment or calls from work to say, "I love you," I tell my sons that this is good. "Remember this for the future," I command. "Emulate this behavior." I'm relentless. "Go shoot some hoops," I said.

End of talk.

Andrew was next. I caught up with him a week after Harold explained sex to him which was two years *before* the school explained it to him and six months *after* he had explained it to his friends.

"Are there any questions you would like to ask me because I'm a woman and might be able to explain a girl's feelings?" I asked.

"As a matter of fact, what do boys do that make girls slap them on the face? How can you tell if a girl likes you? Am I old enough to go to the carnival with a girl unchaperoned? Doesn't French kissing spread germs? How many times did you and Dad have sex? Do you still do it? What if I want to marry someone you don't like? On our trip to California did you get two hotel rooms in San Francisco so you and Dad could have sex? Sometimes when I wake up, my penis is hard. Would you like to tell me why?"

"Do you know that getting flowers can turn a woman on?" I asked.

"Yes," he said.

"Good."

End of talk.

My sons and I have discussed birth control and pregnancy and abortion and date rape and AIDS and abstinence. Sometimes I wait until they ask me a question before I start pontificating. More often I look for a trigger such as a news report or an ad. We've had numerous discussions about what the word "no" means. They know it doesn't mean "maybe" or "okay if you pressure me enough." They know how I feel about women being talked about as sex objects and they don't do it. In front of me. I tell them over and over again that loving relationships are predicated on much more than sex. Either they're listening or I've become white noise to which they are so desensitized that they can make it look like they're listening when they're actually playing telepathic Yahtzee.

Finally I tell them that sex is healthy and fun. Lots of fun. I can see they have a problem with this—not with the message, but with the messenger. I suppose they think it's okay for your mother to have sex, but it's not quite right for her to enjoy it. Despite their discomfort, I keep talking.

When they wanted to learn how to mow the lawn, they watched Dad mow the lawn. And when they needed to learn how to tie a tie, they watched Dad tie his tie. Now they need to learn about sex. They are going to have to do it sans visual aids. All I can do is talk. I have a grand opportunity in my life. More than that, I have a responsibility not only to my sons, but to other women's daughters. Somewhere in my future wait three young women to whom I will give the greatest gifts I have ever bestowed—gifts that have taken all of my adult years to mold. I can touch other women I have never met: teachers and colleagues and employees and waitresses and saleswomen and politicians. I can enrich their lives by raising respectful, egalitarian men. Without ever having a daughter, I will touch many daughters. It is an honor, a calling, and a responsibility. And it begins with teaching my sons about respecting women.

As I was dropping Dan off at a party a few weeks ago, in

an effort to be consistent, I asked him yet again if he had any questions.

For the first time he responded, "Yes, I do. There is something I'm really worried about."

I didn't prod. I waited for him to find the right words.

"Mom, is my hair sticking up in the back?"

Gun of a Son

Boys can kill you and do. Over and over and, in my case, over again. When I returned home from dropping Dan off at his party, I found Harold dead on the kitchen floor. I knew I'd find Andrew dead somewhere else and I did. On the living room sofa. As I lifted his shroud to make sure he'd taken his shoes off before sprawling all over my Prince of Chintz upholstery, I found myself staring into the barrel of a gun. (That is the long, round part from which the bullet is ejected, isn't it?)

"You're not supposed to shoot people before bedtime," I chastised the mass murderer. "You're supposed to play quiet games before bed."

"Dead is very quiet, Mommy." My children are not stupid. "Just die once, Mommy. Just die one more time!"

"Oh, all right. But only because I love you. And because maybe Dad and I can have a conversation in heaven since we don't get to have any down here."

I'm riddled with so many bullet holes you could serve me with ham on rye. Some of the punctures in my body, the perfect circles, were made by super-silent radioactive green laser beams shot from a good half acre away. Others, the scraggly, misshapen wounds, were inflicted by rusty old bullets from timeworn cowboy guns fired at point-blank range. I have had arrows swoosh through my head, knives pierce my ever-lovin' heart, and handcuffs chafe my Oil of Olayed wrists. I've been tied up, burnt down, run over, and plowed through. Just desserts for years of saying I was dying to have children. Now I'm dying in order to please them.

I am a pacifist. (No, really?) Guns scare me. I protested Viet Nam. I made love, not war. When I found out that the woman who cleaned my house packed a gun in her purse, I made her leave her purse in her American car. What I didn't make her do was too much cleaning. The first time she cleaned my house, the process took six hours. The last time she cleaned my house, she was finished in an hour and a half. I know perfectly well that you can do things faster the more you practice them, but I kept having more babies and the house didn't get any smaller and she kept finishing earlier. She stopped vacuuming the living room carpet. I didn't say anything. She had a gun. A pair of my husband's jockey shorts sat in a corner of our bedroom for two months. My lips were zipped. SHE HAD A GUN. I noticed that in a whole year she never ran out of Lysol bathroom cleaner. (She liked Dow better, but I won't use that because Dow manufactured napalm.) I paid her anyway.

SHE HAD A GUN ! And I had a filthy house.

Guns kill innocent people, some of whom are children. One killed the President, which made Mrs. Molser cancel the Brownie meeting that day and we were going to have cake! I leave my front door unlocked. I cry on the opening day of hunting season when they shoot the deer in the park that have been spreading Lyme disease all over the neighborhood. And I forbade my sons (the first two, anyway) to play with guns.

I remember my idealistic "I have the power to shape this child" first-time mother phase. The gun issue is a loaded one and I wanted to confront it wisely and carefully, so, as usual, I consulted the experts of the day, who unanimously agreed that straightforward conversation is the single, most effective way of getting through to your children. I formulated a gorgeous and persuasive presentation geared to the cognitive developmental level of a three-year-old and I sat down with Dan and explained to him that guns are bad. They kill people, and people who are killed can never be alive again. I told him that in our house we celebrate life and love and peace. He responded by shooting me in the eye with his finger.

I remember my undaunted "This is a whole new child" second-time mother phase. Our little family had gone to visit Grandma and Grandpa for a few days. My husband and I stayed in my sister's old room—the Barbie shrine. All of her childhood Barbie dolls, as well as most of the ones she had stolen from me (the originals I might add), were sitting in parallel lines on the dresser like little bald June Taylor dancers. (I used to cut off their pony-tails. The Vidal Sassoon cut was very hot at the time.) Two-year-old Andrew sauntered into our room in the morning and stopped dead in his tracks when he saw the dolls. Reverentially, he whispered, his eyes full of wonder, "Mommy, can I play with those Barbies?"

YES! A nurturer! I wanted to clutch him to my breast and tell him he would always be my favorite child. Instead I said, "Of course, honey. They'd be worth a thousand dollars each with hair, but since they're bald, they're worthless so go ahead and play with all of those beautiful ..." guns. I had looked at the Barbies and seen the June Taylor dancers. He had seen an enormous gun rack. I have to admit that bent in half they did look a lot like pistols. And so he declared a Barbie war. I engaged in Barbie wars as a child, but the battles always involved whose Barbie was going to get to marry Paul McCartney and whose would be stuck with Ringo. The weapons of choice were icy-cold silences or threats of withholding wedding invitations. This was entirely different.

I don't know why little boys are so fascinated by implements of death and destruction. Some people think it's television, but my sons were weaned on "Sesame Street" where no one ever gets shot, and still, when given a choice between playing cops and robbers and playing "Which of these things is not like the other," the bank is under siege before you can say Luis loves Maria.

I could ban guns. I *did* ban guns. But how do you ban pretzel rods, straws, all kitchen utensils, Tinker Toys, Legos, cordless phones, hair blowers, flashlights, ice cream cones, slices of bread that can be bitten into the right shape, markers, pens, cup dispensers, cardboard toilet paper rolls, cardboard paper towel rolls, remote controls, hairbrushes, toothpaste tubes, toothbrushes, candlesticks, candles, Ping-Pong paddles, badminton rackets, toy flutes, chicken legs, sticks, turkey drumsticks, raw broccoli, and baseball bats? And when finally, they use their fingers, do you ban those too?

So I play dead. It's not so bad really. I can do my grocery list, try to remember where I put my keys, meditate, or daydream. I can redesign my kitchen. Hell, I play dead so much I could redesign Tokyo.

Have I mentioned that playing dead is a game in which you can fully participate by not participating at all? I like that. Especially on Sunday afternoons. On Sunday afternoons when mommies of little girls have to play house, which requires lip movement, or board games, which require arm movement, or puzzles, which require brain movement, I can play dead, which requires no movement. I can even play "Shoot me on the subway while I'm reading the *New York Times*," and if I fall face first, I can actually catch a glimpse of a headline or two. The cup is half full.

I've been bonding with my sons for years by letting them kill me. So far, they're happy that I keep coming back to life. Now I'm in my "What's the use, you have no influence over your children whatsoever" third-time book-free mother phase. It's not that I didn't intend to give Zack the gun lecture. I just forgot. Lo and behold, I think he's a pacifist! He's terrified of the vacuum cleaner hose and the hair blower and the woman who used to clean my house, so I fired her. (She didn't shoot me.)

The older two don't play with guns any more. They only play games that have the word "ball" in them. Dan has never expressed interest in owning a real gun, and he wants to own everything. Each October they cover their ears to block out the gunshots on the opening day of hunting season. They even get sad.

Good Night, Zack

Lying with a child in bed is much more fun than dying for a child on the floor, and I have been blessed with the opportunity to enjoy this cozy pleasure every night for the past thirteen years. I've never kissed a daughter good-night. I used to imagine lying under the covers next to a little lavender-scented bundle swaddled in pink flannel and tied at the top with a silver hair ribbon. Sort of like a Fabergé egg. Together in bed, we'd mentally decorate the rooms of our dollhouse or giggle about how the mommies in the TV commercials look so happy when they try a new laundry detergent, or I'd explain how to make a torte. I'd tell her that she's the best friend I'd ever have and she would tell me the same thing and I'd stroke her hair and watch her drift into sleep.

I don't do that with my sons. I lie down next to them on the bed, take a deep breath, and remind them that proper hygiene calls for two teeth brushings a day. They get up, brush their teeth, and return to bed. And then I lie back and let them stroke my hair and tell me how wonderful I am. I am more than their best friend. I am all women. Perfection inside and out. If they'd heard of Catherine Deneuve, I'd be her. In the thirteen years I've been nestling children into bed at night, I've heard the following things.

I am a hot babe.

The only mother prettier than me would be Cindy Crawford if she had children.

I need to put on weight.

I have very soft skin.

I have very soft hair.

I have very soft hair on my skin.

I can make Ellio's frozen pizza better than anyone.

Dad is one lucky guy.

There aren't any girls in the whole school who show any early signs of growing up to be as great as me.

I write better than the dude who wrote "Hamlet."

My brownies are very moist.

I have a better body than Jane Fonda.

I can blow bigger bubbles with one piece of Bazooka than the fourth grade champion can with three pieces.

I don't look my age.

I could pass for a teenager.

I'm very cool because I don't care if kids hear me say the word "bullshit."

I'm very cool because I can listen to a whole Stone Temple Pilots album without throwing up.

What pimple?

I make perfect hot dogs.

I have a beautiful voice.

I'm the only mother in town who sits in trees.

I am Mary Poppins—practically perfect in every way.

I am their best friend.

Last night I received the best compliment of all. Being told by a thirteen-year-old boy that he would like you even if you weren't his mother because he likes you as a person is better than winning fourth row seats to an Eric Clapton concert. And having them pass out free champagne.

At their most wretched, my sons have never said "I hate you" to me. "I hate you" is a mantra for adolescent girls. I have one friend, Julie, whose skin is as thick as an armadillo's because she's had to learn not to crumble from a full year of her daughter Debbie's hurtful diatribes. Harold and I never know from one social engagement to the next in what emotional state we'll find Julie. The success of our evenings together is entirely dependent upon Debbie's fleeting feelings of good will toward Mom. Some of our dates have been like evenings in hell. Or really bad group therapy. We don't hold anything against Julie. Enjoying a filet mignon can be daunting when someone at home has wished that you choke to death on it. After one hour of solitude, Debbie usually realizes that she didn't mean the punishing, accusatory things she said. After one year of therapy, Julie is coming to realize that her daughter doesn't mean the things she said. But after a year, even a great steak is inedible.

I say "I love you" to my boys constantly. For two reasons.

1. I love them.

2. I hear that some men have difficulty saying "I love you" and I don't want to be responsible for bringing three more men like that into the world.

It has worked so far. "I love you" can be taught. All three of my boys can say it to the people they love without gagging. Now I have to worry that they don't say it indiscriminately.

I take comfort in not having to worry each morning about whether today will be an "I love you" day or an "I hate you" day. I am loved every day. The things I say and do, the things I cook, the rules I make are not loved, but I am adored. And at night, in Power Ranger blue instead of pink flannel, with woodchips from the playground stuck between his toes and smelling of sweat, four-year-old Zack lies next to me and we talk about how the Phillies stink this year and we design the fort for the backyard. And I explain how to make a torte.

Then I leave him and weep because tonight brings me one night closer to the night I have to stop. I've already stopped lying in bed with Dan. It began to feel inappropriate when he was about eleven. I may make it to eleven and a half with Andrew. But Zack—the baby I couldn't decide whether or not to have—was not supposed to grow up this fast. As the big boys joyfully meet and greet each exciting new phase of existence, I can't help mourning the phase just passed. Zack has saved his brothers from being smothered by me. Now who is going to save Zack? Someday soon (only a mother who has

been through it before knows how soon) it will be inappropriate for me to lie in bed with him. This is an anguish that only
mothers of sons understand. On visits home I still cuddle with
my mother beneath the sheets. We look at fashion magazines
or old photographs and share private agonies and ecstasies.
My brother steers clear of that kind of intimacy with Mom,
just as my big boys have, one at a time and in perfect, healthy
fashion. Our intimacies will be expressed over coffee or lunch
or at a ballgame, because mommies can't tuck little boys in
forever or rub their tummies until they fall asleep. Thank you
for demanding to be born, Zack. And sweet dreams.

Night Thoughts

In my "not-really-sleep" moments when the boys are dreaming of Heisman trophies to come, and Harold has fallen asleep because he is able to do that without winding down first, I listen to the owl in the two-hundred-year-old oak outside my window, and I relish the tranquil tidbit of time I have to be alone with him and with my thoughts. Sometimes I ruminate over what to make for dinner the next evening. Often I re-live snatches of the day just passed. Occasionally I speculate about what my life would have been without these four magnificent, sleeping men who have woven the fabric of my adult reality.

I'd be single and an urbanite. And probably poor because the ethereal and the practical skills God granted me rarely translate into money. Consequently, I'd be eternally frustrated because what good is being a single urbanite if you can't go out for a nice dinner every once in a while or to the ballet?

I would have pursued a life in the theater that I doubt could have made me fundamentally happy. It is a "Look at me" life. "See, all you strangers, how talented I am, how I can make you laugh and cry by arranging words on a page or by interpreting words someone else put there. Look at me and listen to me and desire to be me and send me your love because I've worked so hard to earn it."

The comedian, actor, and now playwright Steve Martin recently confessed to his own lust for, and addiction to, audience adoration. "The truth is," he said during an interview on National Public Radio, "I spent my entire career in show business begging for the love of an audience. And finally, at the age of fifty-something I have come to learn that an audience cannot send love at all. The most they can send is admiration." Perhaps admiration is all Larry Olivier wanted. Perhaps he was completely fulfilled. It wouldn't have been enough for me.

Nonetheless, unencumbered by carpools and religious school and orthodontist appointments and growing feet that require almost monthly replacement of cleats, I know I would have thrown myself into the surreal world of life upon (or behind) the wicked stage. I would have hung only with other Mamet-ites and Friel-philes. I would have condescendingly looked down my nose at those who don't know Cordelia from Desdemona. I would have lived and breathed the stage until I had no life to imitate, and my art would have had to imitate itself.

Theater is a dangerous drug for me. The highs are celestial and can't be duplicated by ingesting anything so lowly that it has to grow on the earth. I knew this years ago while I wrapped myself in its aura and I know it now while I keep a safe distance from its lure.

The men in my life are not my whole life. A me exists who

isn't wife, mother, or slave. I write and I teach and I lunch with friends and I read. Unbeknownst to them, the men in my life have enriched even those parts of me I don't share with them. Mine is a life abundant with both challenge and routine. My children have given me moments of joy that no theatrical collaboration could equal. They have also opened my heart to the possibility of unendurable pain. Mostly, they make me think every day about how I want to live my life, about where and how we find meaning in this best of all possible worlds, and about how we come to make the choices that once made, carry us to infinity.

The conditions under which I live—the hectic schedules, the catering to the needs of others before attending to my own, the inability to travel whenever I want, spend a whole weekend reading, or get another degree from the college of my choice—make my work more difficult to accomplish than if I had chosen the other path. But the range and depth of the emotions and thoughts that came to me as a result of living with these four enigmas make my work stronger and I think universal. I will never be an artist who suffers in solitude for the sake of my art. I have a built-in, home-grown audience— an audience that showers me with admiration *and* love and even lies if lies are what I need to hear. Wherever I am, I can think of my home and my men, and unlike Gertrude Stein, I know that there *is* a there there. And then I go to sleep.

Morning's Come Up

Zack's toes are little sugar cubes. I know this because they're usually in my mouth for an hour and a half each morning. He doesn't shove his foot into my mouth immediately upon crawling into bed with me. His position of choice is nestled into my armpit with his tousled amber curls tickling my chin. I like this configuration too, although the waking-up experience always has a bittersweet edge just as the bedtime routine does. I dread the first day I miss the sunrise because no short person has tiptoed to the side of my bed to announce, "Morning's come up." On that day my body will ache for the satin cheek, smoother on my breast than my Christian Dior teddy. But then again, I always end up with toes in my mouth.

At 7:00 it is time to begin the "Waking up of Dan" ritual. Because it is the year of Dan's Bar Mitzvah, he is required to attend weekly Saturday morning services. No one I know has heard of a rabbi denying a child his opportunity to become a Bar Mitzvah because of poor synagogue attendance. Even so, I insist that my son live up to his commitment as a Jew, and I enforce the Saturday morning services commandment. My stand against absenteeism necessitated his dropping off the basketball team, but I'm sure that the spiritual fulfillment Dan will attain this year will more than compensate him for any petty sacrifices. I'm sure that of his own free will, Dan will decide to extend his commitment to Sabbath observance in years to come. And I'm sure that cows can fly.

Dan needs two hours to get ready in the morning. One hour and forty-five minutes to wake up and fifteen minutes to shower, shampoo, brush his teeth, comb his hair, don a jacket and tie, locate his missing shoes, eat breakfast, watch a cartoon, make plans for the afternoon, punch Andrew in the stomach, and get out the door.

It is virtually impossible to awaken a teenage boy. I remember this from when my brother was a teenager. I asked our family doctor if they make NyQuil out of some kind of testosterone extract, because the day after puberty hits, boys can't seem to get out of bed. I've called my girlfriends at two o'clock on a Saturday afternoon and have had to apologize for waking up their sons. This inability to come to life in the morning is totally unrelated to how late these boys go to bed the night before. Sleep addiction usually occurs prior to the onset of a social life. Some people believe the simple process of growing up exhausts them. Okay, but if growing up is exhausting, growing old is debilitating, and I still manage to get moving at a reasonable hour. Girls grow up too, and they're usually awake enough to notice. Sometimes on the weekends my friends and their daughters have breakfast together. What a concept! By the time Dan wakes up, I'm ready for cocktails. I usually don't complain. When any one of my children is asleep the house is five or six times quieter than when all of them are awake. I do wonder though if this hormonally triggered excessive sleep pattern in puberty is the beginning of a lifelong fixation on beds, what you can do in them, and with whom.

Getting Ready

No, I didn't make up the "no blue sport jackets with black pants" rule. God did.

When I was young, white socks with loafers was considered nerdy, but go ahead if you insist.

Andrew, you didn't brush your teeth. Okay, prove it.

Because you played two hours of soccer after school yesterday in the mud, and you need a shower.

No, you can't suffocate from a turtleneck.

We just bought those shoes a month ago. Your feet have not grown that much in a month.

Because your sweat stinks! Take a shower.

No jeans in synagogue. Yes he does. God cares.

I can't smell the toothpaste. Brush them again.

Yes, I suppose it is possible to hang yourself using the turtleneck. Are you planning to do that?

No, you don't have to wear a tie if you don't want to.

No, you don't have to button your top button if you don't want to.

Yes, you have to take a shower even if you don't want to.

Yes, the khaki pants are good with the blue sport jacket. I don't know why khaki is good with blue and black isn't. But trust me.

GET IN THE SHOWER!

You're just used to sneakers. Shoes always feel tight after sneakers.

I still don't believe you. Brush them again.

I didn't steal your comb. I have my own comb.

I had gum surgery once. It's the only thing that hurt more than childbirth.

BRUSH THEM WELL! GUMS TOO!

We have to leave in ten minutes. WILL YOU TAKE A SHOWER PLEASE?!

Okay, I promise never to buy you turtlenecks again.

Would you please keep the shower curtain closed? Water is getting all over the floor.

Wear your sneakers, then.

Have you checked out your ears lately? One could light a menorah from all the wax in your ears.

I am not picking on you. I just want you to develop good grooming habits. It's very important.

Okay, I'm picking on you. So what?

Tie your sneakers.

I won't say another word about the white socks. Except this. You look like a nerd.

Yes, we can donate the turtlenecks to the Salvation Army.

Tie your sneakers.

We were supposed to leave five minutes ago.

I'm leaving. Is anyone coming with me?

I'm history.

Tie your sneakers.

Yes, I'll help you with your earring.

A Hole in One ... Ear

The truth is, I not only didn't object to my son piercing his ear, I think I may have suggested it. I'm not sure why. Here's the best I can come up with.

I was too young by about three years to be a real hippie and I've always resented the fact that I missed being part of the Woodstock generation by the skin of my teeth. I wore moccasins and love beads and listened to the Grateful Dead, but I never passed out flowers in Haight Ashbury, or got arrested, and my parents would never have let me go to Woodstock. I missed all the really groovy stuff. So having never gotten groovy out of my system, I do things now like wear beads in my hair (once), listen to the Grateful Dead, and tell my son that it would be soooooo cool to wear an earring.

Dan has a mind of his own and didn't embrace the idea without giving it a good long think. He was torn. He told me he doesn't exactly travel in the earring crowd. I told him not to stereotype people, there's no such thing as an earring crowd, all the while knowing that neither times nor adolescents change, that there is such a thing as the earring crowd, and he's not in it.

I told him to listen to his inner voice, not to let anyone's opinion but his own influence him. I told him that the way he dresses is a personal statement not a political one. I told him it would be interesting from a sociological perspective to see how he would be greeted the day he showed up at junior high with his new gold hoop. And I told him that earholes close up really fast if he changed his mind. In the end it was not his independent, rebellious nature that won out. It was his life-time love of shiny things.

Dan has always been attracted to objects that glitter or glow or glisten. Crystal chandeliers and diamond rings and confetti made of glossy paper fascinate and delight him. He lusted after that little piece of gold in his ear. He wanted to be shiny.

We went to one of the places in the mall where they pierce your ears (or ear) for free if you buy earrings. Dan never looked back. Once he made his decision, he staunchly defended it. Unfortunately, neither of us were prepared for what was to come.

I knew Harold wouldn't like it. I think I even knew he'd hate it. But I also knew that he would not judge or criticize or forbid. Rebellion is greeted with understanding in our house. It takes all the fun out of it to be sure, but on the other hand, there's no motivation for running away from home.

Harold believes, as I do, that matters of personal taste

are not just cause for punishment. He learned this, I believe, from his parents. He and my mother-in-law stated matter-of-factly that they disliked the "look," but that Dan had a right to adorn his body in whatever way he chose. Neither one of them added aloud, "And if your crazy mother allowed you to do this, what can we say anyway?" Dan was safe from criticism on his home turf, as he knew he would be. Sadly, his home turf measured somewhat less than one quarter of an acre, and he couldn't help bumping into the neighbors if he wanted to get some fresh air.

They never used any of the more popular derogatory terms for homosexual or gay, although Dan and I knew they were dying to. Instead they said things like, "Once you wear an earring, it's only a matter of time before you put on a dress." One neighbor said that so often I wished Dan would have pranced around the yard in my tartan kilt just to shut him up.

"I would kill myself if my son went in that direction" was one of the less subtle exclamations aimed at me. Some of the kids called him a girl. It was explained to him by a source he still hasn't revealed, that two kinds of kids wear earrings: gay kids and delinquents. Jocks in earrings don't fly. "Explain Michael Jordan," he retorted. "I've seen him fly!"

I assured him that if we lived in New York, this wouldn't happen, but because we live in a small town, people are suspicious of blatant acts of individuality. There was no need to tell him this. There was no need to comfort him or talk to him about the courage required to become your own person. And there was no need to suggest that he take the earring off. He liked his earring. He didn't buckle under the onslaught of negative judgments. He continued to wear it every day. He wore it to school and he wore it for dress-up occasions. He is wearing it in his Bar Mitzvah portrait. He knows that there are worse things he could be called than gay. In fact he doesn't understand what all the anti-gay sentiment in this country is about. He says he'd be happy if he were banned from the military.

He did wonder about one thing. "What," he asked me, "is the equivalent of a sissy if you want to call a girl something that means she's like a boy?" I was stumped.

"Tomboy, I guess." I replied.

"But being a tomboy isn't a bad thing," he told me. "It's okay for a girl to be a tomboy. Some guys really like tomboys. Tomboys don't get called tomboys in school, and they certainly don't get mocked about it. But being a sissy is really bad. Being called a girl is the worst kind of insult."

He's right. It's fashionable for girls to wear combat boots and bomber jackets and crewcuts. It's even sexy. A woman can wear a man's suit and go unnoticed, because imitating men is flattery. But boys who wear earrings are noticed. Even if they're not criticized, they are noticed. Their motives are questioned as are their identities.

Androgynous dressing has not and probably never will be acceptable to men. Why would it be if it means they'd have to look like women?

Dan lost his earring. He's not allowed to wear it in gym class, and he can't keep track of things that are not attached to his body. No one has commented that he looks masculine without it. No one has called him a stud. I haven't suggested that he get another one. His hole will probably close up and that would be okay. I know that he knows that I know what an independent young man he is. I'm proud to give him to the world. With or without his earring, he shines.

20 Things to Do in Synagogue Besides Participate

If You Are Four

1. Ask if it's over yet.
2. Rip out the fringes on Dad's prayer shawl.
3. Pick your nose.
4. Sing "Jingle Bells" just a bit too loudly.
5. Ask Mom to take you to the bathroom.
6. Go to the bathroom with Mom.
7. Take your shoes off. Hide one.
8. Take your jacket off. Use it for a pillow. Pretend to take a nap.
9. Pretend to wake up. Laugh. A lot.
10. Ask if it's over yet.
11. Tear a button off Mom's dress.
12. Ask Mom to take you to the bathroom.
13. Go to the bathroom with your brother.
14. Ask three hundred questions about things that have nothing to do with where you are.

15. Drop your prayerbook. Preferably onto the foot of the stranger sitting next to you.
16. Roll around on the floor. A lot.
17. Pull Mom's earring until she is in agony.
18. Ask if it's over yet.
19. Bang your head into your brother's stomach.
20. Embarrass Dad until he takes you out of the sanctuary and into the back room for a cookie.

If You Are Ten

1. Ask if it's over yet.
2. Make macramé out of the fringes of Dad's prayer shawl.
3. Pick your nose.
4. Count backwards from three thousand. Out loud.
5. Ask if you can go to the bathroom.
6. Complain about having to wear real shoes. Take them off.
7. Go to the bathroom. Spend a half hour there.
8. Complain about having to wear a jacket. Take it off. Make Mom hold it on her lap.
9. Count the number of ceiling panels in the sanctuary.
10. Ask if it's over yet.
11. Compare all of the people around you to animals. Tell Mom she looks like a camel.
12. Drop your yarmulke onto the lap of the woman sitting behind you.

13. Complain about having to come here in the first place. Inform your parents that this is a stupid activity.
14. Take off your tie. Unbutton your collar.
15. Throw a silent temper tantrum when you are denied bathroom privileges.
16. Drop your prayerbook. Preferably onto your mother's foot. See if you can run her stocking.
17. Ask why we have to come here when we're not that religious.
18. Ask what kind of cake they'll have today.
19. Bang your head into your brother's chest.
20. Make snoring noises during the sermon.

If You Are Thirteen

1. Ask if it's over yet.
2. Play with the fringes of your own prayer shawl. Get your fingers caught.
3. Pick your nose, but make it look like you're thinking about something important.
4. Unconsciously make an origami duck out of a page from your prayerbook.
5. Don't ask to go to the bathroom. Just go.
6. Engage in interplanetary travel. Visit Neptune.
7. Ask Mom if your hair looks okay.
8. Try not to look across the aisle at the girl you have a crush on.

9. Ask Mom if she's sure your hair looks okay.
10. Try to look like you're looking at the rabbi while you're really looking at the girl you have a crush on.
11. Tell your little brother to get out of your face.
12. Take your little brother to the bathroom. Trip right in front of the girl you have a crush on.
13. Complain about missing your favorite television show to come here.
14. Obsess about whether or not your mother is lying to you about your hair looking okay.
15. Drop your prayerbook accidentally. Onto your own foot. Turn red.
16. Complain about having to wear a tie.
17. Count the number of prayers before it's over.
18. Catch the eye of your friend and silently agree to meet afterward.
19. Grab your brother in a headlock after he bangs his head into your chest.
20. Bend down very low, spit into your hands, and try to get your hair to look okay.

I have a theory about why it is that boys are unable to sit still in a house of worship when they can sit for two hours at a Van Damme movie without moving a muscle. It has to do with more than just boredom. I'm no theologian, but it seems to me that boys have a tacit understanding with God that women don't share. Somewhere in their unconscious minds

Oh Boy, Oh Boy, Oh Boy!

they believe that they don't have to work for redemption. Redemption will be granted them by virtue of who they are. They are boys. They can deal man-to-man with God because, after all, he is one of them. And because he is one of them, he must get a kick out of a well-timed fart as much as the boys in the third row did.

Because God is presented to us as a man and a father, girls necessarily must work just a little bit harder than boys to be understood. We women are conditioned to plead for our redemption.

God may empathize with us, but he could never understand us the way another woman can. Our mistakes are not always mistakes that a man can fathom, so forgiveness is a tad uncertain for us. Fear of not being understood is understandable. Fear of not being forgiven can be devastating.

Not being terribly religious myself, for the reasons I have alluded to above, I spend a large percentage of my time in services watching people, and the kid people are the most interesting. The boys, forced into neckties and real shoes, are three quarters of the way undressed before the final benediction. The girls have barely a wrinkle in their party dresses. The sexes are equally antsy to be sure, but more girls than boys seem to try to stay with the program.

I asked my sons for their thoughts and this is what I got.

"In the old days, men were more superior than women. That has changed now, but it's too late to change the Bible."

"The Bible was written by God. God is a man. End of discussion."

"God's job is to make the rules, measure how well you follow the rules, and forgive you for breaking the rules. It's the same as a father's job." To this I responded, "Why can't a mother do those things?"

"She can. Sometimes mothers can do fathers' jobs."

"How would you feel," I ask, "if it was assumed that God was a woman? If all the stories and all the prayers were about God, our mother?"

They thought for a while and gave me a thoughtful and literary answer.

"I don't know."

Well, neither do I.

My Loves Are Blind

When I gave up on advice books about four years ago, I began to read research studies instead. I wanted empirical evidence to support new childrearing theories, evidence particularly related to the care and feeding of boys. Also, since I've never used the *information* I acquired in graduate school in real life, maybe I could at least keep my research skills polished. There is no paucity of recent literature dealing with the differences, both genetic and conditioned, that exist between men and women. Our brains have been dissected and analyzed right, left, and center. Doctors and scientists and doctor-scientists have studied primordial instincts and ancient role distributions and DNA helixes and patriarchies and matriarchies and orientation to math. Here is what I've learned from reading some of these long-winded research reports. Men and women are different from each other. And here is one example of how we came to accept this revolutionary concept as the truth.

An experiment conducted at the University of Rochester

not too long ago involved men and women and observation. One at a time subjects were led to a small waiting room and told to relax and wait for the experimenter to arrive with instructions. What the subjects weren't told was that waiting for the experiment to begin *was* the experiment. The waiting room was strewn with unrelated objects—items such as half-empty toothpaste tubes, stuffed animals, paperback books, pens and pencils and Band-Aids and kitchen utensils and sundries.

After a ten-minute wait, each subject was brought into another room and seated before an interviewer who asked him or her to name as many of the objects as he or she could remember seeing in the first room. Pretty much without exception the women were able to name more than half and sometimes nearly all of the items. Pretty much without exception the men said, "What objects?" The researchers-scholars concluded from their exhaustive scientific investigation that women are genetically predisposed to notice their surroundings and men are not. In response to this ground-breaking twentieth-century revelation, I borrow a phrase from my sons— "No, duh!" Reading *The Firm* was more edifying.

I once spent several weeks of a summer abroad living in a school for the blind. Aside from the obvious absence of mirrors in the bathrooms and a misplaced white walking stick here and there, no clues indicated that blindness was going on inside or nearby. Now I live in a house with sighted people where signs of blindness are clearly visible every day.

In my house, a gum wrapper that has fallen onto the

floor ceases to exist. We have an invisible laundry basket, dishwasher, and trash can. Clothing that gets thrown on the floor because the laundry basket is invisible also becomes invisible. It's all very metaphysical. I used to find it infuriating before I heard about that University of Rochester study. Now I realize it's hopeless. They can't help it. They're born without the power to observe. So I'm no longer infuriated. Just clinically depressed. I'm trying to give them a break and get on with my life. But a question burns inside me like a jalapeño pepper that won't digest. How is it possible not to notice that you've left the toilet bowl full?

Three months ago I underwent nasal surgery to correct a deviated septum. (Yeah, right.) My children had been told that I was going to New York City for the procedure and would spend one night away from home. They weren't worried. I guess they figured if I could survive childbirth three times, I could easily withstand a nose pruning. They kissed me goodbye in the morning and I promised to be home in time for dinner the next day. I kept my promise. I even bettered it. Sporting a rather large splint on my nose, I was home in time to greet them upon their arrival from school. I would think it would be difficult not to notice a woman with an enormous splint on her nose. I was prepared to be gaped at, made fun of, or at the very least, to be asked if it hurt. No gaping. No mocking. No telltale signs of concern on anyone's face. One question did come up, though. They wanted to know what was for dinner. I wasn't hurt or insulted or disappointed. Just incredulous. I no longer expect anyone in my house to notice a change in my hairstyle or a pretty new outfit or a ten-pound weight loss. I did, however, have a splint right in the middle of my face! Maybe they were trying to be polite.

Back to the research study. I don't understand how researchers can conclude from that study that men are *genetically* predisposed to not notice things. The men in the study were all grown-ups. These were not tabula rasas. They'd been subjected to years of mothering. Perhaps they never *had* to notice anything because everything was always noticed *for* them. I might eventually notice a full toilet if no one ever came along to flush it for me. But if it got flushed regularly by a mystical house genie, I might not even realize that I had left it unattended. If by magic, my shirts appeared clean and folded in my drawer every week, I would ultimately stop noticing that they had ever been anywhere else. It would be to my own advantage to do so. And if my own mother slaved in silent acceptance, never asking to be noticed, I would also, finally, fail to recognize her. If I were to spend twenty years not noticing things that cried out for attention, how, once I reached my majority, could I be expected to notice a cluttered mess in an experimenter's waiting room? A cluttered mess is exactly what I had been taught *not* to notice. And at that point, on what grounds do they call my defect genetic? Perhaps mothers of daughters don't slave in silent acceptance. Perhaps they teach their daughters to keep track of their belongings. Perhaps they actually expect their daughters to help pick things up and put things away and they don't expect the same from their sons. This conclusion is even more depressing than the genetic one.

My splint stayed on for a week as the doctor ordered. Okay, I cracked after six days and ripped it off. I looked in the mirror and cried. The face that had been looking back at me for forty years had changed dramatically. Clearly, my nose was no longer boss. It now shared status with the rest of my facial features. There was no mistaking it. I was Audrey Hepburn, only fair skinned and redheaded with a short neck and smaller eyes and a Jewish aura. My mother looked at me and saw the obliteration of a family inheritance. My friends look at me and see a more confident, self-possessed me. And my boys? They saw Audrey Hepburn too, because that is who I told them to see. Right after I told them to see the shoes they had left in the middle of the floor.

Home Is Where the Mess Is

Research results such as the ones that came out of Rochester, though interesting, don't make life any easier to live. Let's say they're right and boys are unable to notice things. Does that mean I have to live a life surrounded by junk? Heelllloooo! I don't think so! Helen Keller was blind and she could set a table. I am not obsessive about neatness. Twenty-five out of thirty days a month, a muddy sock lying on the floor next to the laundry basket instead of inside of it doesn't elicit paroxysms of rage. My back is still strong enough to withstand the effort involved in bending down and picking up the sock. However, a muddy sock that finds its way into one of my Venetian glass goblets acquired impulsively on a trip to Italy ten years ago, and for which I sacrificed a romantic and expensive dinner at Cipriani's—that ever so slightly pisses me off.

Over the years I've instituted numerous tidiness regimes. I tried the reward system first. One day I posted a Brownie point list on the refrigerator door. All household tasks were assigned a Brownie point value. Small, simple, daily tasks were worth two-digit Brownie points, ten points for making your bed, twenty for clearing the dinner table, fifty for putting your toys away without being asked. Bigger, once-a-week chores such as taking out the garbage, cleaning your room, and mowing the lawn were worth hundreds of points. When a chore was completed, it had to be reported to Harold or me. We would record it on the poster. At the end of each month points were totaled. A thousand points would get you a present in the $20-$30 category. Five thousand could get you a really nice gift. Points could be held over from month to month for up to a year. I'm sure Hillary Clinton's health plan was easier to understand and required less calculation. We fought a lot— over such things as how much a chore should be worth, and why the chores assigned to the oldest had a higher point value than the chores assigned to the younger ones. It didn't occur to me at the time that if we were fighting anyway, we might as well be fighting over doing the chores in the first place like we always had, instead of over the silly Brownie point values.

If Dan had a meeting on his night to clear the table, it wasn't fair that Andrew got to clear the table two nights in a row and consequently acquire double points. If I was upstairs when points were reported, I usually forgot to record them when I came downstairs. I'd get caught days later and have to assign an arbitrary number of points, having forgotten who performed which act of cleanliness. And regarding the point system, how do you assign a point value to cleaning melted

Tyrannosaurus Rex out of the microwave or fishing the remote control out of the aquarium? As far as I'm concerned, flushing the toilet after depositing is worth two million points and that takes half a second to do.

I began to feel like Patton. My kids started to look like little Gomer Pyles to me. "I set the table, ma'am," they'd inform me through their vacuous grins. The poster resembled calculus. It gave me math anxiety. And Zack wanted to know why, with all the talk about Brownies, we never had any. Plus, I started to feel funny about rewarding my children for meager participation in household maintenance. After all, they get an allowance just for being alive. No one ever paid me to breathe. The Brownie point system was history in two months time.

During my Catherine the Great period, I instituted the punishment regime. It is, as you surmise, the opposite of the reward system. I figured the reward attempt failed so abysmally that the opposite tactic simply had to succeed. We began to fine the children for any cleanliness infraction. They had to pay two dollars for every time they left the table without clearing. And so on. They quickly ran out of money. I had to buy birthday presents for them to give to their grandparents. They went bankrupt. It's difficult to collect from a bankrupt person. And there was still the math. At least with the reward system I was working with positive integers. Computing negative numbers makes me nuts, and working with bankrupt people necessitates competence with numbers below zero.

Sometimes the boys had decent reasons for being unable to complete their chores. They were fined anyway. They hated me all the time. *I* hated me all the time. The house became a penitentiary. I was a warden. The warden cracked first. End of punishment system.

Attempt number three was the "natural consequences" system. I resolved to not get bent out of shape by the amorphous landfill engulfing me. I would keep my own things clean and neat, and the rest of the family would have to fend for itself. If a new pair of khaki pants sported a chicken parmigiana stain nine inches in diameter and was never put into the laundry basket, then, when an occasion arose that required the use of that good pair of pants, the owner of said pants would have to wear the chicken parmigiana to the theater or party or school function. That person would be subject to ridicule and humiliation, and I would laugh. After all, my pants would be clean. Nice concept. Unfortunately, not one based on reality.

When the choir is all lined up and a huge chicken parmigiana stain shows up in the front row of the tenor section, you can bet the mothers in the audience are not blaming the tenor for screwing up the group photo. They are wondering how the tenor's mother could let him out of the house looking like that. In fact, the tenor probably stands there singing his little heart out, oblivious to the stares of judgmental mothers, while the tenor's mother wishes she had collected ads for a nice program when she had been asked to volunteer for the job, because then at least she'd have something to hide behind.

Another problem with the natural consequences system is that most of the things in our house belong to the grownups. Big things like furniture and appliances and walls are mine. If Play-Doh gets stuck on my wing chair, I want it off immediately. I don't want to wait for the offender to sit down and get it stuck on his cherished soccer uniform while simultaneously pushing the glop further down into my upholstery.

No matter how I looked at it, the natural consequences of filth or carelessness were always mine to suffer. I'm the one who wants to entertain graciously in my beautiful home. I'm the one who has to pay for expensive repairs. I'm the one who should get a master's degree in psychology for the therapeutic techniques I've learned through my feeble attempts to let go of useless attachments to pretty things.

Never a quitter, I decided to shun the ideas of the others and develop my own system. I called it the lowered expectation system. I hear that many children are allowed to keep their rooms as cluttered as they want. They don't get rewarded for neatness or punished for mess. I thought I could live with that. Some parents don't demand that a task be executed to perfection, just that it be done. I thought I could live with that too. I let go of expectations that their rooms be kept neat. I abandoned dreams of finding seven pairs of underpants per child per week in the laundry basket. I even ignored the toothpaste art in their bathroom. Now if I could only ignore the nervous tic I developed from all that ignoring.

This brings me to the differences between clutter, dirt, and destruction. Clutter can be ignored without adverse consequences to the ignorer. Clutter, in my mind, should be listed on the periodic table of elements, although chemically speaking I guess it would be more of a compound. It is a fact of life. Not as vital as oxygen, but nearly as pervasive. In fact, I'm pretty sure that these days even our oxygen is cluttered. There is too much stuff in the world. Everywhere. Until we become more proficient at recycling, condensing, composting, and disposing of our clutter, we will have to be comfortable with ignoring, stepping over, walking around, or decorating it. Knowing this, I am willing to make peace with the clutter in my life. A stray bookbag is allowed to sit on the family room floor for the weekend. I do insist, however, that the boys choose bookbags in colors that won't clash with the furniture. If Zack can sleep better at night knowing that Spiderman is suction-cupped onto the kitchen window, then Spiderman may stay. Unfortunately, you can't do anything about the color of his outfit. It clashes with everything, even itself.

My children have helped me to cultivate an affection for the clutter in my life. I like to think of clutter now as precious priceless mementos of daily life, snatches of childhood and adolescence to keep me company when my children and adolescent are away from home. In fact, clutter is life itself. As a child, my sister used to collect *TV Guide*. At one point I think she had three hundred of them. We lived in a clutter-free home back then, and one day my mother collected the magazines and threw them away. About a year later, I read in the *New York Times* that sociologists speculate that our descendants will learn most about the times in which we now live by studying what we watched on television. In the twenty-second century, *TV Guide* will be a textbook. My sister's clutter, according to this article, was worth a fortune! I am hesitant to accept this as plausible. We already study old TV shows. They're still on. We don't have to read old *TV Guides* to find out what Harriet Nelson wore to cook dinner or how Mary Tyler Moore's job description changed over the years. Beaver is still on TV and still ten years old. And lovable Lucy is still tongue tripping over vege-meta-vitamin. It is possible to watch television twenty-four hours a day and not see anything produced after 1982. But that's a different kind of clutter altogether.

Dirt, although probably as plentiful as clutter, is its own kind of compound. Unlike clutter, dirt can directly affect anyone who ignores it. And unlike clutter, dirt is usually gross. It can get a person dirty. If a person does not want to get dirty, I believe it is perfectly reasonable to ask that the dirt be removed. I don't want Cheerios in my hairbrush or muddy baseball stirrups hanging over the TV, even if they are the stirrups worn while bringing in the winning run. I believe I have a right to object to dirt and I do, loudly and often.

And then there's destruction. Destruction is what separates the boys from the girls. Unlike clutter and dirt, I believe destruction is gender specific. I'll admit that girls can clutter up a house as artfully as boys can. I've been in daughter-only homes and have sometimes been surprised to find them looking even more cluttered than my own. When it comes to clutter, dollhouse furniture, stuffed animals, bottles of nail polish, and beads count every bit as much as matchbox cars, plastic nuts and bolts, and little action figures.

Dirt crosses gender lines as well. A mushy Cheerio is a mushy Cheerio, regardless of whose mouth it's been ejected from. But destruction is a male thing. Simply put, boys are physically stronger than girls and usually have greater upper body strength, enabling them to move furniture with little effort, often leaving huge river-like scratches in freshly finished hardwood floors. I have footprint-shaped holes in my drywall. My refrigerator door is missing its bottom shelf due to being slammed once too hard and once too often. I have a chip in a chip-proof porcelain sink in the upstairs bathroom. The Lladro little boy given to me as a wedding gift by my best friend is missing his hand. Some of the damage is irreparable, some merely expensive. My sons never have malicious intent behind the damage to my belongings. They just haven't grown into their bodies yet. Frequently they are left baffled by the consequences of their youthful exuberance. They wonder why household items aren't built to withstand household people. Uneducated as consumers, they wonder why a sink marked chip-proof can and does chip. To their credit, they regret the damage. Contrition is a hallmark of their creed. Lamentably, an apology won't stick to shattered glass. I know destruction happens in all multiple-boy households. I know a broken lamp is not the end of the world. I KNOW! But I share the space we call home, and I clean the space we call home, and abominations against this space make me NUTS!

Every so often fortitude and perseverance are rewarded in our own lifetimes. I am happy to write that Harold and I finally found a solution that worked and continues to work for all of us. We moved. We moved out of a spanking new contemporary tri-level house into a well-loved and well-worn old colonial. Home now is a two-hundred-year-old stone farmhouse that I believe has withstood even greater forces of nature than my three sons. Chips in sinks are apropos in this house. Distressed furniture is not only acceptable, it's in vogue. How lucky for me to be alive and a mother at a time when our country is "going country."

Woodworkers pelt their cabinetry with chains and double the price. Floor tiles are made irregular on purpose. Painters paint faux cracks in walls. The more my children ravage the premises, the closer I come to a photo spread in *Country Living*.

Still, I am hesitant to display my objets d'art. The large chip in the sink means the sink has history and character. The same principle does not apply to the large chip in Great-aunt Sadie's cut glass punch bowl. That chip means you can't serve punch. I will be fifty-five when Zack leaves home. Harold will be sixty-one. It would be nice to be able to display an antique before I become one.

Thoughts vs. Feelings

The results of another recent study I found fascinating merited a cover story in *Newsweek*. Some people contend that men are born with a narrower spectrum of emotions than women. This accounts for what women perceive to be a lack of sensitivity to their feelings by the significant men in their lives, as well as the complete obliviousness of men to this perception. Researchers testing this phenomenon assembled hundreds of photographs of faces in various emotional states. These photos were presented to both boys and girls. For the most part, girls were able to distinguish subtle variations in mood. They could and did differentiate between surprise and shock, anger and frustration, disappointment and grief. Boys, on the other hand, possessed a limited repertoire of emotional recognition. They were as competent as the girls in determining opposite emotions such as happy and sad, or scared and relaxed, but *degrees* of emotion flummoxed them. Boys could not distinguish being miffed from being enraged, being disappointed from being despondent. What does one do with information like this? If you're me, you conduct your own test.

My goal was more general than the goals of the psychologists cited above. I simply wanted to see what my sons thought about feelings and felt about thoughts. I corralled Dan, my stoic, first. I began by asking him which is more important—thoughts or feelings. He gave the predictable wiseass answer. "Feelings ... I think." This wasn't going to be easy, but I persevered.

"What do you think about the claim that boys and men have a difficult time expressing their feelings?" I asked.

"It's BS. Men express their feelings all the time."

"And what do you think of a boy who cries in front of you?" I continued.

"He's a total wimp and a loser. But no one I know would do that."

"So what you are saying is that nothing really upsetting ever happens to anyone you know? Everyone is happy all the time?"

He began to squirm a little. "No. Bad things happen, but we don't cry about them in front of anyone."

"So your friends express their feelings all the time, just not the sad ones."

He began to squirm a lot. I felt terrible for him. I wondered how anyone could ever consider being a lawyer.

"It depends on what happened to make them sad," he explained. "If someone gets hurt or made fun of, he shouldn't cry, but if his mother dies, I guess I'd expect him to cry."

I took some small comfort in this.

"Would you try to comfort a friend who was crying, or would you be embarrassed by it?"

All-purpose answer. "It depends."

"On?"

"On if his mother died, I guess. Ma, do you want me to fail this math test tomorrow?"

The poor kid was clearly struggling with his feelings about having feelings. I could have pointed out that he's never studied for a math test in his entire life. I could quote him verbatim, "It's impossible to study for a math test!" But the pain of watching him sweat was too intense and I terminated the interview. After all, I had obtained the information I had set out to obtain. I just wasn't sure what to do with it.

Andrew was next. As I had predicted, the responses of my most labile son were diametrically opposite to those of his brother. Andrew believes it is okay, even healthy, for boys to cry as often and as loudly as they want. And he practices what he preaches. But Andrew is only ten. Dan cried when he was ten, too. And Andrew is toughening up by the day. His brother has been working on him. By the time he is thirteen, I'm sure he too will be a bundle of contradictions. He too will have mixed feelings about having feelings.

I'm Dan's mother. I've seen him cry. I know the things that will make him cry and they are not always personal attacks or losses. He cries at "E.T." every time.

And Dan is wonderfully adept at giving comfort. He has consoled me on several occasions. He doesn't get disgusted looking at a runny nose. He's generous with hugs and kind words. And yet, he is noticeably uncomfortable acknowledging that this is a part of him that makes him special and cherished.

What happens to our little boys? They are being brought up by mothers—intelligent, modern mothers. Do mothers allow their daughters to own their feelings but force their sons to dissociate from theirs? The subjects in the above study were six years old and older. These boys had already been exposed to society's expectations. Were they born able to distinguish variations in feelings and able to express a broad range of emotions? Do we teach them with every passing day that this is unmanly? My babies have always been sensitive to subtle changes in mood. They didn't particularly enjoy nursing on days when I was anxious or depressed. As young men they seem to have lost some of this sensitivity.

If I tell them that I am anxious or depressed, they are more often than not generous with their love and support and willing to accommodate me. But they must be told. They are not attuned to subtle emotional temperature changes.

It is possible that my children are embarrassed by my labile nature. I do have a tendency toward overreaction. An air of mystery has never been one of my attributes. I can't help it. I'm prone to bursts of elation and fits of angst. On more than a few occasions I have gotten myself into trouble by feeling before thinking. But just as often, the honesty of my emotion has been appreciated by those who find mystery a drag. No one ever has to guess why I am angry or disappointed. It makes getting on with things a whole lot easier.

Can feelings be taught? I think we can learn empathy by watching positive interpersonal relationships occurring between the people who are significant to us, but I'm not sure it is possible to learn to have feelings that you do not possess. Unfortunately, we can and do learn to suppress feelings that have never been acknowledged or validated. I assure my boys that they don't have to worry about turning into me if they allow themselves the chance to connect with their emotions.

I'm growing up with my sons. I've seen their toddlers' temper tantrums give way to the sulking, pouting, and crying jags of childhood. Now I am experiencing the silence of adolescence. It's a killer. When the baby whose every need you've attended to, whose every tear you've wiped, whose every anxiety you've assuaged closes the door to his soul even temporarily, you feel deserted and somehow belittled. You want to be the same cushion against misery that you have always been, but their silence flattens you and their desire for an untouchable, private self seems as inconsiderate to you as it is healthy.

I've encouraged my sons to open themselves to all kinds of emotions, to let their feelings flow freely from their hearts and spill over onto those they love. I've taught them that pain hurts and that the free expression of that hurt is what sets the healing process in motion. They have learned that joy is twice as sweet when one has experienced sorrow. And I have learned that the life lessons a mother shares with her children during their early years evaporate in the heat of teenage conformity.

The experts would have us believe that our children return to us with open hearts when adolescence has had its way with them. Maybe. But it can't ever be the way it was. Nothing ever is. I used to think that was bad. But I have learned from my sons. As a person who has spent years training herself to be more circumspect about where and to whom I express my innermost feelings, I now feel that a little withholding can be healthy. Perhaps I should learn to be more temperate as I teach them to be more expressive.

Everyone has lived for a time inside of a woman. Most mothers relish the symbiosis. Once our children are separated from us physically, our bonds become emotional ones. We itch to know every sentiment that passes through the hearts and minds of our sons and daughters. And more than that, we long to share those sentiments ... feel them. We can't. Especially not with our sons. We can only think about what they must feel. And that feels ... unthinkable.

He Ain't Heavy, He's My Little Brother

*O*r maybe my boys do express their feelings openly and regularly, and it is my own limited comprehension of their language that's the problem. I have yet to attain fluency in wrestle-ese. I continue to assume mistakenly that anger or jealousy are the ingredients that provoke a heated session of roughhousing. You would think that by now I'd have come to understand that sometimes they kill each other out of love. If I expended as much effort on interpreting their swats and swipes and wallops and slugs as Jane Goodall spent learning to interpret the body language of chimps, perhaps I'd be able to distinguish an affectionate blow to the head from a hostile one. Frankly, I'm not interested in spending that much time with them.

For years I let the roughhousing get to me. It would break my heart to hear Andrew beseech Dan to play with him.

"I'll play anything you want," he would grovel just to get a shred of attention from big brother.

"But Andrew sweetheart, Dan's favorite game is folding you up to see if he can fit you into the dryer. Don't you remember how your knee got stuck in your mouth the last time you played with him?"

"It was fun, Mommy!" Translation: Being origami for Dan is preferable to being invisible to him.

Logic suggests that Zack would be afraid to get near his big, huge brothers when they wrestle. He doesn't get near them. He gets into the middle of them. He specializes in headbutting. Like a battering ram, over and over again he thrusts his little head into Dan's stomach until Dan flips him like an omelette and tosses him to Andrew, who gets him in a choke hold and tickles him until he can't breathe. This is bonding behavior of the highest order. Zack has finally become one of the guys.

I saw a cartoon in a magazine, which I cut out and hung on my refrigerator door. Two boys were wrestling on the family room floor. Arms and legs were flailing everywhere. Their mother shouted, "SOMEONE IS GOING TO GET HURT!" To which the older child responded, "Of course someone is going to get hurt! How else would we know when to stop?" Well, how would they?

I've been very lucky. No bones have been broken yet. Windows, chairs, toys, lamps, Harold's glasses, the Ping-Pong table—all have been casualties of the melees. But my children have remained for the most part intact, so I suppose they are signaled by something other than catastrophe that it is time to cease and desist. Peeing seems to work nicely. If someone pees in his pants from laughing too hard or overexertion, the conflagration instantly loses its glamour for the other person. Tears work well also. There's no joy in beating a person to a pulp if he's going to cry about it. Beware of generalization, though. All moisture isn't the same. Sweat *enhances* a good brawl. Mothering boys has helped me overcome any queasiness I may have once had to disgusting fluids like pus and snot and blood. Now I can dress a wound while watching "Seinfeld" and eating potato skins. I don't let run-of-the-mill nosebleeds interfere with a phone call, and I know what kind of music to play to keep a child awake after a concussion.

My sons learned the joy of being tossed around like little beanbags as soon as they could hold up their own heads. Men seem to delight in heaving their tiny sons into the air and catching them. And in an infantile act of kindred spirit, boy babies whoop with glee, encouraging Dad and all male visitors to throw and catch, throw and catch, throw and catch over and over again until moisture appears. Then Mom comes in for the wipe. My friends who have daughters tell me that their husbands never confused the baby with a basketball. Their girls were danced with and twirled, but never lobbed. Laura's daughter was thrown once but didn't give a reinforcing yelp, so she has been pretty much earthbound since. Harold still tosses Zack into the cathedral part of our cathedral ceiling, but he can no longer lift our older sons. On land. As soon as they are in a pool, a lake, an ocean, the throwing of children

begins again, and the hollers and whoops of the pure, un-
bridled joy of being tortured resound for miles. Roughhousing
in an ocean can continue indefinitely. An ocean, after all, is
moisture. No one will know if you pee.

I can do nothing to stop the private, physical communication that passes between, on top of, underneath and inside
of my sons. They can no more stop wrestling than they can
stop growing. If Dan couldn't punch Andrew in the shoulder,
how would Andrew know that Dan's day sucked? And if Andrew couldn't respond by kicking Dan in the behind, how
would Dan know that Andrew's day wasn't so swell either?
Without the punch and the kick they wouldn't have the intimacy that comes from sharing a bad day.

I wouldn't think of forbidding them to emote physically
when they have positive feelings to express that they are unable to share verbally. There are times, however—many, many
times—when war breaks out for reasons that have nothing to
do with bonding. For example, Dan has a habit of clonking
Andrew on the head every time a TV commercial interrupts
the program he's watching. He's never angry; he just wants
to use up the thirty free seconds he's got on his hands. Andrew, after enduring years of this torture, has learned to an-
ticipate commercials and now ejects himself from the sofa
and out of the room seven or eight times a half hour, knowing
that Dan won't clonk him if it means he has to get up.

Long car rides provide ideal conditions for physical activity. My kids have learned to execute perfect somersaults and

backflips without ever unfastening their seat belts. A game of Twenty Questions can easily deteriorate into a riot when one of the questions asked by Dan is "Is the person you're thinking of as ugly as Andrew?" They've played car football without a football and car basketball without a basketball. They are capable of such feats of contortion and endurance that I can imagine the finesse they'll exhibit with other physically intimate activities when they are old enough to take their dates out in cars unchaperoned.

Despite frigid temperatures, snow days can be hell. Two years ago, during an ice storm, when mothers were stranded at home for three weeks unable to get out even to pick up videos and Ritalin, a local psychologist appeared on television every evening at ten to offer friendly tips on what to do with your children to keep them happily occupied during their confinement. I think someone shot him. I wished it had been me. When boys can't get out for air, they go berserk. You can bake brownies or put puzzles together or play bingo or even stage the family Olympics, but when two o'clock rolls around and they haven't been outside, the house turns into an arena that makes Madison Square Garden sound like a library. They kick and scream and roll around like dervishes until they exhaust themselves or hurt themselves, whichever comes first.

Why do psychologists think that given enough constructive activities, children won't drive their mothers to distraction? Mothers are driven bonkers every day by children who are all but drowning in Play-Doh and construction paper and glitter and glue. When was the last time that TV shrink was housebound for two weeks with his kids? He certainly wasn't stranded during the blizzard of the century. He was sipping coffee at Channel 10.

My friend Amy has grown sons. She says when they get together, they wrestle for old-times' sake. She says it does her heart good to see that they still love each other enough to slug it out. She'd like to remove the wall-to-wall and refinish the beautiful hardwood floors underneath. But she can't. What if they come for Thanksgiving? Someone could get hurt.

Louisa May Who?

When "A Little Princess" opened at a theater near us, I received numerous invitations from well-meaning girlfriends. In voices pink and thick with pity, they generously asked me to join them and their daughters on this eagerly anticipated cinematic outing. I could have seen the movie with seven different mother-daughter duos had I been so inclined. But I was inclined to decline. The movie opened and closed, and I, in my martyrdom, missed it because I didn't want to be a third wheel on a special mother-daughter date.

As little girls, my women friends and I had been entranced by the classic Shirley Temple film of the classic Frances Hodgson Burnett story. There is something terrifyingly romantic about orphanhood, and I pretended to be poor Sarah Crewe for a full year after experiencing the movie magic. I never imagined myself as the wealthy, couturiered Sarah, but rather was compelled to enact only the days of hunger and mistreatment. I remember stealing charcoal briquettes out of our backyard grill and carrying them around in a bucket, certain that Lavinia would be demanding a fire in her bedroom momentarily. I remember fantasizing that it would be truly wonderful to have your father die so everyone who ever treated you badly would feel sorry for you and sorry for what they had done or said, and then, after a little while passed, to have your father magically return as an amnesiac who, upon hearing the sound of your voice, would instantly recover his memory and resume his previous existence as if nothing had ever happened. "A Little Princess" was a memory too beloved to share with just anyone. I could not horn in on that kind of mother-daughter bonding experience. Anyway, I was certain my friends had offered to include me only because I had told them in great detail about my trip to Broadway to see "The Secret Garden" with my sons.

I've tried to put the experience behind me. It's been several years now, but something in my heart still hurts. "The Secret Garden" is another cherished children's story. I was not surprised when it was adapted for the musical theater, and I was thrilled for the opportunity to share this heartwarming fiction with my children. The boys are not readers, avid or otherwise, so I look for alternative ways of sharing literature with them. The original book was short on action, but I figured that singing and dancing are their own kind of action, and that at the very least, the choreography would be enough to sustain the boys' interest and keep them still for the two hours they would be confined to their seats.

It cost us $280.00 for four tickets. (Zack hadn't been

born yet.) Plus tolls. Plus parking. Plus lunch. Plus the snacks we bought them at intermission to bribe them into staying for the second act. Recently my husband and I were asked by a friend to name the three people, living or dead, whom we respect above all others. I listed Ghandi, Shakespeare, and the stranger who sat behind Andrew at "The Secret Garden." Watching Andrew during the opening strains of the show was a little like watching an early Robin Williams stand-up routine. At that time, Robin Williams had drugs as an excuse for his freneticism. Andrew's only excuse was Andrew. He performed gymnastic feats in his chair that Mary Lou Retton would have found impossible. Had I been the one who paid seventy dollars to sit behind him, I'd have used my *Playbill* as a mallet before the overture ended. Fortunately for everyone around us, Andrew fell asleep halfway into the act, and to this day his only memory of the experience is a stiff neck.

Dan was older and more civilized. Under his breath he found every word in the English language that rhymes with boring. Some aren't very nice. In sotto voce he asked me what he had done to be punished in this way, and if he promised to stop doing it, would I promise to keep him away from Broadway forever? I was devastated. Aside from the fact that my dream has always been to live and die on Broadway, this wasn't just Broadway, THIS WAS THE SECRET GARDEN, DAMMIT! YOU'RE SUPPOSED TO LOVE IT!

I was a self-pitying wreck for weeks afterward as I diligently attended to the task of repressing the whole experience. I tried to resign myself to a lifetime of Arnold Schwartzenegger movies. Naively, I had assumed that once my children's taste in media matured beyond the Ninja Turtles, I would be able to share Audrey Hepburn with them. Yeah, right.

Ever the good sport, I've slept through more action-adventure movies than most of my friends know exist. I don't mind that Sylvester Stallone has made a several-million-dollar-a-movie name for himself. He's the American dream incarnate. I don't even mind that my children admire him. He works hard. And he ... well, he works hard.

I do mind that they admire the characters he plays and the characters Bruce Willis plays and even the characters that "Ahh-nold" plays—the gun slinging (or whatever technological masterpiece of weaponry they sling in the twenty-first century), fast car driving, womanizing, muscle men whom we call heroes. Where are the real movie heroes these days—the Mr. Smiths who go to Washington or the Spencer Tracys of Boystown or Dagwood or Moses? Where has Moses been lately? Campaigning for the right wing, I think. I have sons who need someone to admire besides Bruce Lee. In my life before motherhood, I studied child development and television in graduate school. I believe that watching too much violence can indeed cause people to be violent. But putting that incendiary issue aside, I still cannot understand a nationwide fascination with the underside of life. I am more comfortable letting my sons watch movie scenes of sexual intimacy (within reasonable parameters) than I am letting them watch bullets fly into people's brains.

The following quote is from Jack Nicholson. He says, and I paraphrase, "If you kiss a tit (personally I prefer the word "breast") the movie will get an R rating, but if you chop the tit off with a machete, the movie can still be rated PG." This doesn't make any sense to him and it doesn't make any sense to me. Does it make any sense to ANYONE?

Fortunately, my sons have their other favorite movie genre to turn to on the occasions when I deny them the senseless violence of action-adventure. Unfortunately, this genre is brainless comedy. Fortunately, I'm not insulting anyone by labeling these films in this pejorative way because, unfortunately, the producers, directors, and the writers themselves use such titles as "Dumb and Dumber" or "The Stupids," knowing full well that stupidity sells. What is a mother of sons to do?

Movie going is one of life's great equalizing experiences. I imagine that I have nothing in common with the Queen of England other than the configuration of our internal organs and the fact that we both have divorced people in our families. But if I ever should be seated next to her on a plane, I know I can break the ice by asking how she liked "Sense and Sensibility." Denying my sons access to the movies would be as regressive as sending them to school in knickers and knee socks. They'd be cinematically challenged pariahs. No can do.

So, as with everything else, I talk to them. I point out the curious phenomenon that Sean Connery at sixty-something can still have onscreen romances with twenty-something women, while Elizabeth Taylor is allowed to do that only in real life, never onscreen. They're too young to get it. They still prefer teen-something women.

They have commented that costume budgets in recent years must be higher for men than for women because women are required to wear so much less. I tell them that lingerie can be very expensive. It's all very depressing. Or it was until I remembered "E.T."

Dan, back when he was Danny, cried at "E.T." I rented it and showed it to the other two. They cried. Danny, now Dan, cried again. So I put my toe into the water.

I rented "The Wizard of Oz," which they had loved in their nongenderized days. They loved it again. And then I waded up to my ankles and tried some never-before-seen movies. "The Sound of Music." They liked it a lot, but would I please not tell anyone.

"Exodus." Big hit. I began to feel that I hadn't been giving them enough credit.

We decided to try a movie outing and let the parents select the movie. We hadn't tried this in quite some time. We took the two older boys to see "*Apollo 13*." Victory was ours. No chair gymnastics. No mental mind-twisting games. No hejira to the bathroom. They sat still in public for close to three hours and watched a history lesson. And they learned about real heroes. I definitely hadn't been giving them enough credit.

Only the orphan test remained.

I rented "Oliver." They loved it. But it was about boys. "Annie." They liked it and watched it twice. It was a terrible movie and a giant step backward. "Father Goose" came next. It was a keeper. But it had Cary Grant in it. An unwritten cinematic law rules that people of all age, race, class, and gender must love Cary Grant. I had reached the final hurdle. Terrified that my new hypothesis would never become theory, I nevertheless rented "A Little Princess" two days after it came out on video.

"Whatever you do," I admonished them. "Don't laugh. I don't think I could handle that."

They didn't laugh. They didn't move. Zack sat in one position so long his foot fell asleep. They didn't cry. Neither did I. But they liked it. They liked it a lot. So much that I caught them watching it for a second time the next morning. And why not? It was a terrific movie. With or without Cary Grant, everyone loves a terrific movie.

I berate myself for believing that there are such things as boy movies and girl movies. There is only boy crap and girl crap. A great movie or a great play transcends gender. Those who believe that action-adventure is for men and romance is for women are crap-oriented. Thank God my children are not. They still watch garbage, and it sometimes saddens me to see them enjoy it. But in my depths I know that they know what an elevating experience a superior movie or play can be, and they instinctively know how to discern.

And in my depths, I do remember that "The Secret Garden" we saw on stage that day, was, in fact, a crushing bore.

I Can Do Anything Better
Than You. And I Do.

All four of my men say I'm not competitive enough. I give up too easily. They may be right. I'm sure it's not because I'm a woman, but because I'm me that I'm unable to experience the exhilaration of a hard-won fight. I can't even be competitive with myself. I stop exercising before the endorphins kick in. In fact, I'm not sure I *have* endorphins. It's not that I'm not a fighter. I think my battles have been quiet, invisible ones. I pick them or they pick me carefully, and I fight valiantly but without a lot of noise or action. Not so with my three little hellions who greet each new day as a new opportunity to score points, gain leverage, take the lead, and emerge victorious by sundown.

My friend Edye taught me the remedy for the "He Got a Bigger Piece of Cake Than Me Blues." If you let one child cut the cake and the other choose which piece he wants, you can be sure that the cake will be cut evenly. Edye has a daughter and a son, so I suppose that fighting over who gets the biggest piece of cake isn't a male thing. But I think breaking the wrist of the person who gets the biggest piece of cake might happen more frequently in boy-only households.

I exaggerate. In my house, no one has ever intentionally broken another person's wrist over a perceived inequality. But contusions, lacerations, abrasions, and malocclusions are not uncommon occurrences.

I never expected life in our house to be like a sojourn at Walden Pond. I knew early on that noncompetitive learning experiences were probably going to fail, but I had no idea that in a houseful of boys, passing the salt can be an Olympic event. It's not that my sons are unwilling to stop and smell the roses. They are. Provided that the person who finds the most aromatic rose wins a prize.

Competition around here goes well beyond who can run fastest, jump highest, or hold his breath longest. Any activity can be adapted for competition, including sleeping. Despite my noncompetitive nature, I am able to understand the motivation behind certain contests. Whoever makes it to the shower first in the morning takes the hottest shower. The intrinsic reward for the victor merits the exertion it takes to get out of bed early on frigid winter days. But there is no reward for being able to hold two hundred and seventeen pieces of popcorn in your mouth at once. Moreover, there is no call for this skill in life. What is to be gained in terms of ego strength for the winner of the most humongous oral cavity contest continues to elude me.

Andrew has always had a slight pessimistic streak. Since the day he was born, the sky has been falling, and any day now it will probably land in his lap. I have great difficulty reconciling this personality trait with the fact that he continues to think he can conquer Dan in a contest based solely on brute strength. Like the optimistic child who feels certain that Dad hid a pony in his pile of manure, Andrew continues to arm-wrestle his big brother because he's sure those Wheaties he ate for breakfast are going to kick in any minute. It hasn't occurred to him that Dan has always been older, bigger, and stronger. I gently suggest that he might want to postpone physical competition until they are both fully grown. He worries that they might not want to wrestle anymore by then.

Dan has always enjoyed winning. I don't understand how he gets satisfaction from winning the "Who Can Name the Most State Capitals Contest," when he has studied the capitals in Social Studies and Andrew hasn't. Half the fun of winning, I explain to him, is outsmarting a formidable opponent. I gently suggest that he postpone mental challenges until Andrew has caught up to him in school. He worries that they might not want to play mind games by then.

I deduce from these exchanges that my sons are simply unaware of ways of playing with another person that don't involve competition. They ask me to name one.

"House," I say.

"House?"

"Yes. You've never heard of playing house?" I begin to

hear myself sounding like an idiot.

"You mean like pretending stuff? Is that what you mean?"

"Never mind." I was defeated. I couldn't think of one thing that my kids would enjoy doing with each other that was totally noncompetitive.

Education is a wonderful thing. When Harold and I put our overeducated heads together sometime last year and called on our vast store of collective knowledge, we achieved mutual epiphany. It was as good for me as it was for him, and it was this:

Nothing we can do can change the basic personalities of our children. It is up to us, their loving parents, to devise coping strategies for ourselves in order to avoid bloodshed. Most haven't worked. Here are some that have.

1. Never judge a competition, particularly when scoring is subjective. On snow days when schools closed, I used to conduct the "Family Olympics." We began with the passing of a candle and ended six hours later with a ceremonial extinguishing of the flame. In between we played checkers and coin toss and Simon Says and Hangman and poker and I can't remember what else, but I was always the judge and many of the competitions were judged subjectively on a one-to-ten scale. Kids get wise to you when you try to keep the score tied or in favor of the younger or weaker child. They hate that. Wars can erupt when the players suspect that the judge is either partial or impartial. War is not something you want to have inside your home on a snow day.

2. Apathy is good. Never get too excited about a win or too devastated over a loss. The response that works best for me is, "That's nice (or "that's too bad"), go wash your hands, we're eating soon."

3. Flipping a coin to determine who goes first is a nice idea but can easily go awry when the fur flies over who gets to be heads.

4. Don't waffle. If the oldest child receives a larger allowance, a later bedtime, a bigger room, it's okay. He's the oldest. But he should also have a greater number of chores and responsibilities because he is the oldest. You know what is fair. If you're not sure, pretend you are. This is when people who weren't too embarrassed to play pretending games in childhood have the edge.

5. Don't mediate. If they must compete, let them agree on the rules, the rewards, and the penalties.

6. Instead of cake, buy cupcakes.

More Night Thoughts

In my "not-really-sleep" moments when the boys are dreaming of ways to kill me because I wouldn't let them go to the Phish concert unsupervised, and Harold is tossing and turning and passing wind in bed because of my fabulous chili, I listen to the owl in the two-hundred-year-old oak outside my window, and I relish the tranquil tidbit of time I have to be alone with him and with my thoughts. Sometimes I ruminate over what to make for dinner the next evening. Often I re-live snatches of the day just passed. Occasionally I speculate about what my life would have been without these four time-consuming, energy-sapping men who have woven the fabric of my adult reality.

I'd be gorgeous. I could go bra-less if I wanted to because my breasts, strictly ornamental, would still have the energy to fight gravity. Stretch marks to me would be what happens when you awaken on your yacht and while stretching accidentally scratch your cabin wall with your diamond.

I'd be rich. Dating Prince Albert of Monaco can do that

for you. I'd be bored by the Cannes Film Festival by now, but not by the cooking classes I take from Patricia Wells in Provence. A perfect duck confit is always a thrill.

I'd be enviably well read from all that time spent on airplanes and on the beach. My cocktail party conversation would be scintillating. I'd be able to quote Euripides in Greek and not care that nobody cared.

I'd be free to worry about how much snow was going to fall on Aspen this year instead of whether or not my grandchildren will have clean air to breathe and Social Security.

I'd dine with Walter Cronkite and Al Pacino and the Dalai Lama and they would grill me about what I would do to achieve peace in the Middle East and how I would cure AIDS and how long I thought JFK Jr.'s marriage would last.

But I wouldn't be on Broadway or Off. That would be too farfetched.

Male-Nutrition

This chapter is about feeding a teenage boy. It is also the only chapter for which I have curbed my natural tendency to hyperbolize. Today (truthfully) Dan ate:

Breakfast at a diner

> One twelve-ounce glass of orange juice
>
> One eight-ounce glass of milk
>
> Two scrambled eggs
>
> A pile of homefries
>
> Two pancakes
>
> Three sausages
>
> Seven pieces of toast

Snack

> Five Oreos
>
> One eight-ounce glass of milk

Lunch

> One triple decker sandwich made with one half-pound of turkey breast and one half-pound of bologna and one quarter-pound of cheese

One-half of a giant-size bag of tortilla chips
One cup of salsa
Six Oreos
One quart of iced tea
Snack
The remainder of the giant-size bag of tortilla chips
One cup salsa
One quart of iced tea
One apple
Snack
Two Ho-Hos
Sixteen ounces of milk
Dinner
One roasted chicken
A plateful of French fries
No vegetables
Two lettuce leaves
Half bottle of Paul Newman dressing
Early-evening snack
The rest of the Oreos in the bag
One twelve-ounce glass of milk
Late-night snack
One large frozen pizza with pepperoni
One quart iced tea
I could say more but why?

Lookin' Good

I believe Kate Moss wears a negative dress size. My most petite girlfriend wears a size two, and from what I can tell from recent photographs, Kate is thinner than she is, so the designers must make her clothes in negative sizes. I'm not jealous. I'm old enough to be Kate's mother and I've got nothing to complain about. I look damned good for a forty-one-year-old woman who has borne three children. What I'm complaining about is how much work and sacrifice it takes to look this good, which is good enough for me but not good enough for Kate, so I can only imagine how tedious her life must be.

So let's talk about Goldie Hawn, who is fifty or almost and a far more realistic role model for me than Baby Kate. Since the release of her movie "The First Wives Club," every woman in the country over forty (and many under forty) aspires to look like Goldie. I read somewhere that Goldie eats no dairy, no wheat, and no sugar under any circumstances ever. That means she doesn't inject chocolate during PMS attacks. She's unmoved by the baguettes at the boulangerie in

Paris. She doesn't crawl into the refrigerator when her heart is broken. She said "Never ever" in the article and I believe Goldie. Her autopsy, and I hope she lives to be a hundred and ten, is going to reveal nothing but bottled water in her system. Goldie also exercises like a fiend. Women who have maids and home gyms can do that. I don't begrudge Goldie her maid or her home gym or her great tush. I wish that all women had equal access to a tush like hers. In a true fitness meritocracy, self-discipline would be the only thing that separates the rest of us from Goldie. Unfortunately, in the real world, genes have a lot to do with it too.

Body image is one of the few but burdensome resentments I carry with me regarding being a woman. I bear enormous hostility toward our ubiquitous media that unrepentingly advises us that to be beautiful we must chisel away at our bodies until we attain the physiques of twelve-year-old boys. I am the media's darling, a quintessential chump. I can track the hate-hate relationship I've had with my hips back to the day Twiggy ponied her way from Carnaby Street into the pages of *Seventeen* and *Vogue*. I've spanned the alphabet on diets from Atkins to the Zone in my quest for the elusive size-four figure. And I'm genetically thin! If I'm a neurotic mess about this, I shudder to think about the wounded psyches of my lovely size-fourteen sisters, among whom was Marilyn Monroe.

I can recall dozens of intimate chef-salad-hold-the-cheese-dressing-on-the-side lunches with my teenage girlfriends during which we would fantasize about being boys. Boys could eat hamburgers for lunch if they wanted to. Boys didn't have to fast all day if they thought they might have a sundae after the movie date. Boys didn't have to hold themselves up to ideals that can only be achieved with an airbrush.

Now I have boys, and after a decade and a half of observation, I realize how absurd those adolescent musings were. Body-image demons raise their hideous little heads in the homes and hearts of growing boys with as much conviction as they do in girl-dominated environments. The havoc they wreak is no less debilitating. The only difference is in the icons. In our home the icons are not emaciated (a more accurate word for female models than the euphemistic "waif-like," which has become a semantic staple in fashion magazines). In our home the icons are pumped up. They are Michael Jordan and Arnold Schwartzenegger and Sylvester Stallone and Steven Seagal. My kids implore me to squeeze their biceps and punch them in their stomachs. Dan's latest quest is for a washboard abdomen. They worry that they are too thin (not true), too short (definitely not true), and worst of all, too weak (so untrue as to be absurd). I try to tell them, as I munch on carrot sticks, that physical fitness is important, but bulging muscles are compulsory only for men who aspire to become action heroes in the movies. Or rock stars, I suppose. Women like a well-built rock star. Despite the fact that Michael Jordan is gorgeous, you don't have to be gorgeous to play ball. God knows baseball players don't win any Mr. Universe pageants.

All mothers know their children are beautiful and tell them so or should. But the media are more powerful sometimes than even a mother's love. My sons are not simple-minded, although even if they were, they would be able to glean from television that the big, strong hero always gets the girl. They see who gets to karate chop the bad guys into a pulp. And thrill of all thrills, they see who gets to fly. It would be unusual if they didn't want to physically emulate those superheros, both real and animated, who repeatedly save the world while looking sexy and desirable in their form-fitting costumes.

Over the years a few noble attempts have been made to create strong, powerful, female superheros for little girls to admire. Linda Carter couldn't salute the flag without her breasts falling out of that strapless all-American uniform; how could she possibly raise her arm high enough to take a swipe at a space invader? It's a wonder "Wonder Woman" survived a single season. "Charlie's Angels," the mega-hit of the early Seventies, produced a generation of girls who, rather than registering in droves for fitness classes to become strong and agile like the three supermodel actresses, instead scurried like lemmings to beauty salons to buy Farrah Fawcett's hairdo.

Today we have more educational television fare, such as "Baywatch," which, by glorifying both female and male bodies, has done its part to transform the quest for beauty and fitness into a unisex pursuit. Women are no longer content merely to fit into a size-four silk chemise. Today it is essential that abs of steel ripple through that size-four silk chemise, which should be sleeveless to permit an unobstructed view of the biceps. Today's man craves big pecs *and* Farrah's hair. We're all of us crazy. Boys and girls. Men and women. And we all know we're crazy and we all know what the media does to us, and despite this we keep adding channels to our cable systems and decorating twelve-year-old girls to look like twenty-five-year-old vamps in our magazines, and we put men on billboards with open flies. As we create our idols, so do we create anorexia and bulimia and insecurity and neurosis and failure. Only our therapists profit. And frankly, none of them look like Bruce or Demi either.

The Naked Truth

It took much longer than I thought it would take to write this book. It took a year and a half. It didn't take nearly as long as I thought it would take to bring a child to the age of fourteen. It took an instant. Since the day I first put fingers to keyboard, my sons (from youngest to oldest) have developed bladder control, biceps, and facial hair. I surprise myself each morning by not weeping at the hum of Dan's new electric razor. I've accepted the fact that each of them will leave me in due time for avenues open only to the young and unencumbered. What I am less able to reconcile is the fact that they will leave me for other women. I am unable to fathom that women will become desirable to them. They still pant over the neighbor's golden retriever, Jenny. They lavish her with their full glossary of compliments and would rather spend their beach time romping with her than ogling the bikini-clad beauties who set up fort nearby. Unfortunately, it wasn't Jenny's picture that showed up on my computer screen this morning when I turned it on to begin a chapter about—I forget what.

Nestled amidst the icons for various databases, half-finished articles, and assorted reading-readiness programs, were icons titled simply, "Jessica," "Nadine," and "Mona." Since no one bearing those names lives here or has access to my computer, I was curious about who the owners of these files might be. So I opened one. I wasn't spying. Each of my sons has a folder with his name on it, and Harold and I respect their private jottings and correspondence. I opened "Jessica" because I thought someone named Jessica was borrowing my computer space. What I found was a color photograph of Jessica, stark naked and well oiled. I don't think she was there to introduce our new automated checkbook. When we purchased this computer, I insisted we buy a user-friendly machine because of my incompetence with all things technical. Well, I must admit, Jessica looked very user-friendly. The users, however, were not going to think the same of me. Heads were going to roll.

For several months I've been trying to download photographs of Oklahoma in the 1890s for a new project I'm beginning. I can't do it. I'm either going to have to hire someone to help me or get my rear end to a library with a Xerox machine. How did my sons figure out how to download pornographic pictures? These must be even more challenging to obtain than pictures of the Oklahoma homesteaders, yet the boys had managed to clog my screen with several of them.

I didn't and don't know how to react. My body broke into a sweat as I pictured my babies drooling or worse over Jessica and Nadine and Mona. I was saddened by what I perceived to be a precipitous end to their innocence. I was angry they had the nerve to post those pictures in my small plot of cyberspace. Those women share my hard disk with all of my feminist writings, my plays about women, my personal letters to my friends. I suppose a part of me was relieved that my sons take delight in the female form, but that was tempered with a dose of resentment that they too will come to believe that in order to be beautiful, a woman should look like Jessica. And finally, I was able to see the humor in the situation. They got caught. They were either too naive or too out of their minds with lust to take the time to hide the photos in their personal folders. Now they were going to have to face "the mother," Jessica's antithesis.

Coming to terms with our sons' sexuality is a daunting endeavor. I remember—we all remember—squirming at the thought of our parents engaging in sexual activity. I was sure mine had only done it three times, once for each of their children. The thought of them naked together nauseated me. Today, as a parent myself, my mind is more willing to accommodate that ludicrous picture than it is to play host to visions of my sons as lovers. I hope they are gentle and respectful and giving. I hope their lovers are women with whom they've established a strong, mutual affection. I hope they accept the fact that most women are physically imperfect. We have freckles and poor muscle tone in places and hips a little too large or breasts a little too small. And we are still beautiful. Jessica and Nadine and Mona are not making it easier for us. Neither are the women in the *Playboy* magazine I found under the bed. Do boys grow up thinking so little of their mothers' house-keeping that they believe that the floor underneath their beds never gets dusted?

Harold contends that punishing them will give them the wrong message. The only thing they did wrong was getting caught. How do I respond to that? Is it, in fact, healthy to gape at naked women? Very few of my junior high school friends gaped at naked men. I don't think any of us did. Our passions were for men who *did something* and were cute— like Paul McCartney or Bobby Kennedy or Bruce Jenner or our best friend's cousin. It was a package deal. We weren't attracted to nameless, naked bodies.

I'm fairly certain that my sons will not grow up to be misogynists or rapists. And if they do, God forbid, it won't be because they gaped at these photos. I can make a stink and stop them from engaging in this activity on my computer, but I can't stop them from doing it altogether, just as I can't stop myself from being embarrassed and a little angry about it. So Harold will have another talk with them about exploitation and Dan will point out again that these women do this volun-tarily and get paid handsomely and is that really exploitation? And Harold will hedge and the boys won't stop looking at the pictures because they know their father did the same thing when he was fourteen. And life will go on.

I've decided to keep my mouth shut so they will continue

to do their "boy thing" in my house, where they know that the woman who lives here is embarrassed and a little angry. Here they will have to learn to be discreet. That's the best thing I can do for them. Next to pressing the delete key over Jessica's name.

Kimmy

Well, I don't have to worry about Jessica any more. Now I have to worry about Kimmy. Kimmy is real and fourteen and adorable and Dan's first girlfriend. I worry about Kimmy, but not because of what she might do to my beloved son. I worry about her because of what my beloved son might do to her.

At the risk of making this sound like therapy, my adolescence sucked. I was a hundred feet tall by the age of twelve. Not the way Brooke Shields is a hundred feet tall—more like the way Jeff Goldblum is a hundred feet tall. I had short, curly red hair in 1968 when fashion dictated long, straight, and blond because that's what Jean Shrimpton had and she lassoed Paul McCartney. To make matters worse, I wore glasses and was the editor of the school newspaper. Not surprisingly, Mary Tyler Moore was my steady Saturday night date.

Self-conscious and awkward, I avoided all co-ed events except for the two hundred Bar Mitzvah parties my mother made me attend after having gone to the trouble of forcing her friends to force their sons to invite me. Fortunately, my wallflower soulmates were also there under duress, so I was never at a loss for comrades-in-whining in the ladies' room. Dance cards were de rigueur in those pre-consciousness-raising days. When the boys who were scheduled to dance with me chose to disappear temporarily into the bowels of the synagogue or country club, I was no more humiliated than I was relieved.

I wallowed in self-pity for three years. Halfway through high school, the boys matured enough to ignore people they didn't like rather than torment them, and my spindly arms and legs assimilated into the rest of my body. What doesn't kill you makes you stronger, and I count among my rewards for having lived through those horrendous years a fierce independence, a complete disregard of physical appearance when forming relationships, and a vast storehouse of empathy.

Unfortunately, but I think understandably, my natural inclination with regard to teenage relationships is to empathize with the girl. Women of my generation who never spent an ungorgeous or unpopular day in their lives also empathize with the girl, and not only because she shares our gender. We came of age in a time when the boy asked for the date, the boy paid for the date, the boy requested the second or third or fourth date. Homecoming queen or wallflower, bookworm or socialite, we measured our worth on a scale created by men that, thank God and Friedan, is now antiquated but still exists in our existence, forever bending our sympathies toward our little sisters.

Poor Dan shoulders the burden of every date (I did actually date starting in about eleventh grade) I ever had, real or imagined. Women have remarkable memory with regard to their past loves. Twenty-five years later, I can still envision the paisley miniskirt and go-go boots I wore to see "Five Easy Pieces" with Daryl and the orange floral Nehru jacket with bellbottoms I sported to see the Rolling Stones concert with Bruce. Wouldn't it be nice if feats of memory like these could get you somewhere in life? I have total taste recall of the meals I ordered on dates, I can draw the furniture arrangement in my boyfriends' houses, and I can recount conversations verbatim. But more significant than any of that is the file I maintain in my cerebral cortex that contains accounts of the injustices I've collected over the years in case I ever want revenge. The boys who have offended me or hurt me or ignored me are listed alphabetically in my mental Rolodex. Luckily for them, revenge is not my style. Learning from experience is, and that is where Dan comes in.

I implored Dan on the night of his first school dance to ask the tallest girl in the room to dance.

"You don't know what it feels like to tower over all the boys," I explained. "You feel so … conspicuous."

I told him that making fun of the way a girl looks is grounds for castration, and if I ever heard that he did that, he'd be smart to hide the knives. I admonish him not to lead a girl on, to always be honest and forthright. I explain how easily the hearts of fourteen-year-old girls can be broken.

Kimmy has no idea what a friend she has in me. I'm her secret ally working behind the scenes to ensure that her experience with my son is a positive one, or at least as painless as an adolescent romance can be.

Is there a father at Kimmy's house doing the same for my Dan? Is there someone who, by virtue of his own experience as a male adolescent, is telling Kimmy to be honest and forthright with my son? Will he tell her the truth about how easily the hearts of fourteen-year-old boys get broken and how very difficult they are to mend? Will he tell her stories about his own insecurities as a teenager and about how nervous Dan must be each time he asks her to a school function? I hope so, but I doubt it. My guess is he'll say, "Haveagoodtimebehome byeleven," and leave it at that. He'll worry about whether or not my son will get physically aggressive. I'm sure he's taught Kimmy how to say no and given her a quarter for an emergency phone call. Daddies are too protective of their little girls to worry much about the psyches of their little girls' dates.

It would be nice if Kimmy has an older brother, a boy who has already weathered the *sturm und drang* of teenage relationships. If that's the case, I can count on Kimmy's mother to teach her to be sensitive to Dan. Only after you've been intimately exposed to life on the boy side, do you understand how truly fragile these bulky beings are.

I'll watch out for you, Kimmy. I promise. Now be good to my boy and break up with him gently. I'm not quite ready to be replaced.

Now You See It ...
Now You Still See It

Magic feeds my body and my soul. Extract it from my bone marrow and I'd be left anemic and automatic and dreamless. If I didn't truly believe that one day Tom Cruise would appear out of thin air at my local grocery store, what reason would there be to wear lipstick to squeeze cantaloupes? Magic to me is the same as optimism. It is what Samantha Stevens, the beautiful, blond witch, could weave on television: enchantment that could make even the most hopeless or ridiculous situation wind up better than okay because not only did you get to be right, but you got to be right in a beautiful taffeta dress. During my aforementioned adolescence, which sucked eggs, I incessantly fantasized about being endowed with Samantha-like powers. Wouldn't it be the ultimate if I could twitch my tiny little nose and miraculously be asked to dance at the eighth grade graduation ball? Wouldn't it be even more wonderful if I could twitch my nose and miraculously give myself a tiny little nose? Disney is partly to blame for my perpetual reveries. All of those fairy godmothers and Tinkerbells waving wands and sprinkling fairy dust can really play head games with real girls whose feet could never contort enough to fit into itty bitty glass slippers. To be fair, Cinderella and her counterparts were around long before Walt got his hands on them. Generations of women have grown up repressing their hunger to believe in princes on white horses, but nonetheless longing to believe. Our idea of magic has nothing to do with our own active involvement in it. The magic of our youthful fantasies requires no intelligence, dexterity, or training. The prerequisites to qualify for wish granting have to do with being very pretty, very unfortunate, very helpless, and in dire need of a handsome prince who is not repulsed at the thought of kissing a comatose stranger. Passivity is paramount. Magic is done *to* us, not *by* us.

Samantha Stevens outclassed Cinderella not only because she had a last name, but because she was able to perform her own witchcraft. As prescient as this was in a prefeminist culture, it wasn't truly liberating. Samantha was forced by her husband to keep her powers under wrap. He refused to marry her until she promised to stop plying her trade. So in love was the poor girl that she vowed to live out her days as a mere mortal with a man who wasn't a prince, but a bungling fool and not even cute, which gave new meaning to the phrase suspension of disbelief. Women viewers *had* to believe in magic in order to accept that a witch as bright and beautiful as Elizabeth Montgomery could fall in love with such a bombastic klutz. But I stray.

The point is that when you are a little girl, you don't think about things like activity versus passivity or fairy tale archetypes or feminist theory. You just wish you could be Cinderella. Magic is living happily ever after.

Magic for boys is making the Statue of Liberty disappear. Magic is pulling the right card out of the deck or making a quarter fall out of someone's ear or filling a cup to greater than its capacity.

Every boy I have known has gone through a magic phase. Dan is fourteen now and still in his. He has been playing with cards and quarters for eight years, and his fascination with sleight of hand shows no sign of abating. When Harold and I see him approach with a deck of cards in hand, which is often, we brace ourselves for a long evening. (Should he ever get mugged, I shudder to think of the vengeance his attacker could wreak upon discovering that the rectangular wallet-shaped contour on Dan's back pocket is not created by a wallet but a deck of Bicycle playing cards.) If there really is a sucker born every minute, I've been reincarnated twelve thousand times by now. I beg to be released from this torture, but I am never freed. "Just one more trick this is really cool you'll never figure out how I do this" is crooned almost nightly in our house. If, horror of horrors, I do figure out how he does it, I am sentenced to watch the same trick performed countless times until it can be executed to perfection. "David Copperfield couldn't do better himself" is his victory cry. In our house, David Copperfield rules.

Why, I wonder, is it "beyond cool" to be able to make it look like the Statue of Liberty has disappeared when everyone knows that it is, in fact, still there. For the same amount of money and energy could Copperfield make O.J. Simpson disappear? Now *that* would be providing a valuable service.

Perhaps a fundamental difference between the sexes is that girls want magic to make nonexistent things appear, such as engagement rings. Men, whom we know to detest system overload, are happiest when they feel uncluttered. The more things you can make disappear, and the bigger those things are, the better your life.

Magic for women has always had to do with relationships. (Like something hasn't?) We bask in the magical transformation of Eliza Doolittle from guttersnipe to princess, but we revel even more in the fact that she eroded the defenses of a confirmed bachelor in the process. Women delight in the alchemy of two souls melding. Men prefer to marvel at the magic of the starship *Enterprise* in all of its high-tech impersonal gadgetry and glory.

A feeling of being out of control induces a girl to flee into daydreams of magical resolutions. And the feeling of controlling attracts boys to perform feats of magic. Unfortunately, magic can manipulate only objects, not relationships, so girls abandon magic early on because of its uselessness. Objects are attractive to boys precisely because they are easier to manage than people, so magic holds its allure for them for a good long while and sometimes forever. What could be a greater show of control than making the Statue of Liberty (a woman, by the way) disappear?

My kids always insist that I watch them perform. They make me rate their dives off the diving board as if I were an Olympic judge. I watch them shoot baskets and I count how many seconds they can hold their breath and I attend American Education Week and watch them participate in class. I watch their soccer games and their tennis matches and their holiday pageants. And I don't mind any of it. I'm a non-judgmental, easy-to-please audience. I'm an audience who allows "do-overs" and missteps and comic antics. Something is always gained in the performance process. They develop strength or coordination or stage presence or insight. I haven't yet figured out what Dan gains by forcing himself on me night after night, trying over and over again to put one over on me. Perhaps ego strength, although it has been evident since birth that he wasn't shortchanged in that department. It is difficult for me to be gracious about watching new magic tricks. I find myself wishing Dan would disappear. Or wishing that a princess on a black stallion would come and sweep him off his feet so he could put magic behind him once and for all.

If No Means No and Maybe Means No, What Does Yes Mean? Maybe No.

And now, for my sons, the story of how Grandma and Grandpa met. It is one of their favorites.

Once upon a time Grandma and Grandpa were working together in Baker's Shoestore. In those days Grandpa's name was Al and Grandma's name was Phyllis. Al was a shoe salesman and Phyllis was the cashier. This was interesting and unfortunate because Al couldn't care less about shoes and Phyllis couldn't care less about numbers. One day, between fitting shoes and punching numbers, Al politely asked Phyllis for a date. She politely declined, claiming that she was practically engaged to a nice young man with much better prospects for the future than a mere shoe salesman could ever imagine. Okay, so she wasn't so polite. Never one to take no for an answer, Al waited for a few days and when a second opportunity arose after all the shoes had been fit and all the numbers had been punched, he asked again. Again he was rebuffed. Undaunted, with nothing to lose and Great-grandma's cooking to gain, he persisted, begging over and over again for a casual date and swearing that all he sought was friend- ship and a potato latke or two. Never one to stand between a painfully skinny person and a latke, Phyllis invited Al over for dinner. The rest is as predictable as a Fred and Ginger movie plot and the menu at the Carnegie Deli.

Grandpa, who never sold another shoe after that dinner, believes there is a lesson to be learned from his personal boy- gets-girl triumph. "If I hadn't persevered, if I had crumpled from rejection, you wouldn't be here today," he boasts to his grandsons.

"If I do what you did, Grandpa, I could get arrested!" Dan replied the last time he was regaled with the greatest love story to come out of Rochester, New York, since Bausch met Lomb. "If a girl says no to me, I'm not supposed to keep bothering her. That's called sexual harassment."

He's right. By today's guidelines my mother was harassed. She married my father. Today she would have sued him. I've told Dan and Andrew time after time that no means no. I've also told them that maybe means no. And that sometimes, if the girl is either not very nice or totally confused, yes can also mean no. I assumed they were perplexed. I was prepared to write about how muddled up all of this is and about the rapidly swelling gray area that exists between romance and harass- ment. In search of quotes I broached the subject this morning, and to my surprise it appears that my sons are not perplexed at all. They are resolute about never asking a girl out again after she's turned them down once. When asked about the dreaded kiss good-night, Dan said that if he had a rousing good time on the date, and if he was, in his own words, "without a reasonable doubt" that the girl also enjoyed herself, he would test the waters by bestowing a tiny peck on her cheek. If she didn't hit him or slam the door in his face, he would know that the next time he could get a little closer. Any girl who dates one of my sons is going to have to beg for a decent kiss, so afraid are they of recrimination. The time-tested slap on the cheek is no longer considered ample punishment for perceived sexual harassment. My sons are used to hearing words like trial, fine, witness, and testimony, and they are used to hearing them on the evening news. Regular people make headlines for violating the personal space of others. Recently, regular people included a little boy who was suspended from school for planting a kiss on the cheek of his first-grade crush. My children would prefer to grace the national news for other reasons, mostly having to do with sports.

I have been rewarded for my parenting efforts by having sons who understand the importance of respecting the boundaries of the young women they will encounter as they make their way in the world. It is a world hobbling under the amorphous weight of political and social correctness. We must try to establish a reasonable size and shape for this weight in order for our sons and daughters to be able to bear up under it. Had the onus of sexual harassment hovered over my father almost half a century ago, I would not be here today to tell my sons to beware of it.

My mother admits to having reveled in the attention of her courageous suitor, the kind of possessed lover my sons can never be. Their girlfriends' wishes will be respected regardless of whether they are perceived to be valid. I am proud of them for that. I am also glad that these girls are too young to remember the look on Scarlett O'Hara's face the morning after Rhett Butler wouldn't take no for an answer. That would confuse the hell out of them.

Sons of the Beach

My older sons and I took separate vacations this year. To the same place. At the same time. In the same rented beach house. To my dismay, time and place were the only elements of our vacations that coincided. For the first time in sixteen years of married life, Harold and I accepted an invitation to vacation with friends. We are people who enjoy our privacy. We feel that traveling with five people is an act of courage. Traveling with ten must be an act of lunacy. But we've known and loved these friends for eleven years. Their collective neuroses are sympatico with our own, and besides we could afford a nicer beach rental together than we could if we lived in separate cottages. One more mark on the pro side of our pro-con debate factored heavily in our decision making. David, the Dad of our companion family, is an athlete. He plays tennis and basketball proficiently and isn't chopped liver in the baseball or Ping-Pong arenas either. My sons would romp in sports heaven in his company. Off the beach. On the beach they have their father.

Harold transmogrifies on the beach. Free of his suit, tie, and calendar, he could be Frankie Avalon's stunt double. (I myself, in my new Gottex, look rather like Annette Funicello's grandmother.) Harold's disinclination toward acts of athleticism on land completely belies his prowess in the water. Three years shy of fifty, he can body surf with the fifteen year olds— better than the fifteen year olds. And far longer than the fifteen year olds. Immune to the wrath of Neptune, he challenges breakers that send lesser men racing for their paperbacks and piña coladas. He has inspired awe in his sons. And one step past awe is emulation. My full-time beach activity is counting heads as they bob in and out of the waves.

I was thrilled that my children would be entertained on both land and sea. But that was before I realized that I would be spending the week without them.

I suppose there are women who enjoy an afternoon of body surfing. There are women, after all, who enrolled in The Citadel. I know there are women who are exhilarated by a good, sweaty game of basketball. They are growing in number rapidly. I am also well aware that tennis is a passion shared by thousands, maybe hundreds of thousands of women my age and older. I wish I could be one of those women. I've lost many lunch companions to the sport. I wish that God would have endowed me with an athletic gift for something, anything besides speed diaper changing. It's not that I haven't tried. True, I haven't persevered, but I feel you shouldn't have to work as hard on your recreational activity as you do on getting through medical school. There is a theory that if you put chimpanzees in a room with typewriters for a long enough period of time, eventually they will write "Hamlet." I guess if you put me on a tennis court for fifty or seventy years, I might be able to make contact with a ball. But "Hamlet" is the greatest play ever written and I'm talking about hitting one lousy tennis ball. Just so I can play with my kids. I don't think so. So we take separate vacations together.

During the day they play in the water and they play basketball and tennis and Ping-Pong and all sorts of other things that require eye-hand coordination. Now and then they say "Hi, Mom" as they race past me. In the evenings we have dinner together and they talk about the waves they caught and the shots they made and I congratulate them. Every third day or so I ask one of them if he'd like to go for a long walk. I seem to be able to walk for long distances fairly competently. Once in a while one of them will go for a short walk with me as a warm-up to preferred activities. I thank God that I have healthy, exuberant children who enjoy challenging their bodies as well as their minds. And I thank God I have Zack. Every year on our beach vacation I make a gigantic Mickey Mouse in the sand. Zack is the only one who still likes to help. Zack still likes to hold my hand in the water and chase gulls down the beach. He needs me to wipe the sand from his eyes and to baste him in sunscreen. Once this year, he fell asleep on my lap wrapped in a towel. But the enticements of "big-boydom" are seductive, and the desire to be one of the gang

more heady than even a mother's hug. Last year he was afraid
to go into the water past his knees. This year he proudly stood
chest-deep. I cheered for him even though I knew that I face
total abandonment in the near future. I've envied women on
the beach who finish entire novels in a matter of days. Now
they look forsaken to me. They must be the mothers of sons.
I watch the mothers of daughters. They read, but their bikini-
clad offspring lie not too far away on blankets, listening to
their radios and watching the boys who have left their mothers to cavort in the water.

Our friends have a son and twin daughters. Their son
joined the men at play. On occasion, their daughters joined in
as well. But the girls also found pleasure in a leisurely walk on
the beach with their mom. They required assistance twice daily
in getting a comb through their tangled hair. One night their
mom, my friend, sat cuddled with one of them in an easy
chair, lazily and contentedly combing her daughter's hair for
an hour or more. How jealous I was as I watched my tangle-
free kids watch the US Open on television.

On the last afternoon of our vacation, the girls realized
that they had yet to buy their souvenir tee-shirts and trinkets
for their friends at home.

"Please, Mom, let's go shopping," they begged.

The words fell on my ears like needles. Off they scurried
in memento-frenzy. They asked if I wanted to accompany
them, but I declined.

Inviting disappointment, I walked out to the beach and

asked if anyone wanted a tee-shirt.

"Yeah, Mom," they responded. "Pick out something for me. We're going home soon. I wanna catch one more wave."

And that's the best and the worst thing about having boys. There's always one more wave.

Solitary Confinement as Fact of Life

So it boils down to this. Fear of abandonment. Mothers of sons have it and mothers of daughters don't. I hope I'm right. I hope I'm not the only mother of sons who suffers this ever-present affliction. That would make me feel hopelessly abandoned. I confess to being a little on the pathological side, because my nightmares about abandonment in old age began in first grade. In these vivid dreams I would always be tied into a wheelchair in the dark. I was invisible to my sleeping self except for the shimmer created by my silver hair. Someone had left me in a strange place, alone and shivering and frightened. I had the faintest glimpse of the pristine place from which the angel of death beckons, and I longed to go there, but no one was with me to wheel me across the border of the land of the living, so I had to wait. I was forced to wait for an eternity to be taken to my eternity. I'd awaken clammy and cold, and I'd lie still like that, like a stone waiting for an eternity, until Mom would come in and turn on the light and tell me to get ready for school.

This dream recurred throughout my youth and much of my young adulthood, planting deep in me a terror of being abandoned. Fortunately, this has been balanced by a potent lust for adventure, and I have never allowed my primal fear to keep me from taking risks or forming intimate relationships. In fact, I'd kept my demons at bay for so long that by the time I formally interwove my life with Harold's, I thought I had this abandonment thing licked. And then we had sons.

My brother loves my mother unreservedly. From three thousand miles away. He didn't move to the opposite coast to get free of her, but neither did he stay in the Northeast to be near her. He tries to remember to call her once a week. He succeeds in remembering to call her once every two or two and a half. When she craves his presence because my father is in the hospital or because someone has reached a mile-stone birthday or anniversary, he invariably comes home. But she knows less about his daily life and he less about hers than either of them knows about Princess Di's. This is okay though, because my mother has daughters.

My sister lives five minutes from the home in which we grew up and maintains an active, almost daily role in nuclear and extended family matters. Her family joins my parents for dinner at least once a week. She happily runs errands that my mother is either too busy or too tired to accomplish, and she can be counted on to take part in celebrations, even for birth-days that aren't divisible by five. She is the most likely one of us (though I hope to be beside her) to hold Mother's hand and stroke her hair at the end. I live seven hours away by car, visit as often as my sons' athletic schedules permit, and am in touch by home phone, car phone, e-mail, and beeper. It is not unusual for me to talk to Mom three times in one week even on slow news weeks. Sometimes a daughter needs help deciding what to wear to a dinner party. Sometimes a mother needs to know what was served. My mother is continuously aware of my comings and goings, my tragedies and triumphs, and how my jeans fit. She is an endearing presence in my children's lives. She hears the report card grades and the soccer scores and what an abomination my last haircut was. She doesn't even know if my brother still *has* hair. This doesn't encourage me to contemplate my future optimistically.

Our family dynamic is not unusual. Writers and comedians have made fortunes illustrating the precariousness of the mother-son relationship. Before I ever had that boy twinkle in my eye, I shuddered at the stereotypical portrayals of overprotective, demanding Jewish mothers who molded their sons into wimps if they stayed close to home or ogres if they left. Shelley Winters in "Bye Bye Birdie," Philip Roth's Mrs. Portnoy, Woody Allen's entire oeuvre—any boy with even a shred of a hope for psychological health would be wise to flee from these women. But my mother is not like these women and her friends are not like these women and still their sons leave, not always in the geographical sense but almost always in the emotional sense. It is a disgusting fact of life. Sons leave.

As if that isn't a large enough pill to swallow all by itself, women are forced to face another indisputable and disgusting fact of life. Husbands die.

According to statistics I have a far greater chance of being widowed than does my husband. The many reasons for this phenomenon include the fact that most husbands are older than their wives, which holds true in our house, but so what? It is still going to hurt. I have grudgingly resigned myself to the fact that Harold will leave me someday. I pray that it will be when he is ninety-six and I am ninety and I pray that by that time I will have three dynamite daughters-in-law who will be as diligent about coercing their husbands to stay in touch with their mother as I am about seeing to it that my husband stay in touch with his.

I am curious about (actually I fear) what my sons will tell their wives-to-be before we are introduced. I suspect that I will not be faced with the challenge of living up to a picture of perfection painted by worshipful children. It is far more likely that I will have to prove myself a contradiction of my sons' caricatures. So be it. I am equal to the task. I have to be because the little ring placed strategically on the left hand will dramatically and forever shift the balance of power in my family in favor of the woman who wears it. The proverbial ball will be in my court. I will be responsible for forging a loving-but-not-smothering, helpful-but-not-invasive, mature-but-not-patronizing relationship with my daughters-in-law. The painful truth is that it doesn't matter whether or not I like these women.

If I love my sons—and I do—if I want them to welcome me into the lives of my grandchildren—and I do—if I want them to want to include me in the joys and sorrows of their life cycle events—if at last I want them to walk me into the waiting arms of my angel, I will have to suck up. Pride be damned. The power to let go once and for all of a lifetime of abandonment issues no longer rests solely on my shoulders. The power lies dormant at the moment in the hands of three young girls from who knows where, whom I have yet to meet. I hope they'll like the sweaters I'm knitting for them.

The Importance of Being Dad

The truth about being men slaps you in the face as it announces itself. Only men know what a man is and how to be one. I have a clear and exuberant vision of the men I would like my sons to become, and it saddens me that while I can set them on an honorable path, only Harold can accompany them on their journey. They may seek my advice and have, in a million matters having to do with everything but the essence of their existence. Questions about their manhood can only be addressed by Dad.

As a child, Harold was unlike any of our three treasures. Disinclined toward any sports, he played folk music and presided over his synagogue youth group. My sons have been frequently and unabashedly disappointed that he is not the kind of Dad who plays catch or football. He doesn't even watch other people play football on television. He is the kind of Dad, however, who escorts his sons to sporting events because he knows they enjoy that activity. He is the kind of Dad who enthusiastically attends every one of their games, who cheers for their victories and aches for them when they are defeated. He is a Dad unafraid to show love physically, verbally, silently, and constantly. He shows them by example how to honor and respect all people, but especially their mother. He shows them that the measure of a man is not in his biceps, but in his deeds.

If all women could be led by their heads instead of their hearts, all children would have such role models. I was not such a woman. It was dumb luck that my head fell into agreement with my heart on the subject of Harold. I did not marry him for reasons so sensible or calculated as wanting to provide our future children with an apotheosis of a father. I married him because he was really cute. Plus he treated me well.

Harold has helped me navigate the waters I swim in with my three little monkfish. Sometimes it feels like we're swimming in circles. I will never understand what it feels like to be a boy, and I have no hope of them ever understanding what it feels like to be me. Dan read my essay about our beach vacation and thought I was criticizing Andrew and him for deserting me in the sand. I had to explain that it was sadness, not anger that informed that piece. And Harold backed me up by further explaining that their mother tends to be hypersensitive to flagrant demonstrations of growing up.

My sons, through a combination of luck, effort, time, and devotion, are flourishing and maturing into young men who are enchanting companions. People seem to give me credit for this. I suppose it is natural for people to lavish praise on a mother when her children seem comfortable and content in their skins. As much as I'd like to accept the accolades, the truth is, Harold often makes me look good. I don't coast around here. I put in my late nights and suffer my migraines and anxieties and teach whatever life lessons I have the chutzpah to teach, and I love them to distraction, which gets me through more than a few well-intentioned screw-ups. Single mothers raising boys are unsung heroes. They face challenges they couldn't have imagined as young women and they meet them bravely and often alone. In a perfect world each one of these women's sons would find a male role model in an uncle or a teacher or a neighbor or a coach. I wish that for all of them. Even in my most prideful moments I know that my sons' souls were first God's and now Harold's to shape, and I am blessed to be able to entrust him without reservation with my legacy.

Bashing Bashing

I confess to having participated in a fair amount of male-bashing. It's easier than tennis and sometimes it's even fun. But male-bashing loses its allure when you become the mother of sons. It is one thing to cry "All men are rats!" after a series of horrific blind dates and quite another to do it while baby men are twisting their way out of your body. I already said that I believe in sisterhood. I used to think the term meant the bonding together of women in mutual distrust of men. Now I see that each time a woman disparages the opposing gender, she disparages the children and husbands and fathers of her sisters. That doesn't feel like loyalty to me. In the name of sisterhood am I supposed to apologize for bringing three more men into the world? How can I carry within me a rage against the male animal and still be capable of expressing a natural and profound love for my own sons and their father? The contradicting efforts would paralyze me.

Every day women are battered and neglected by beings of the same gender as my children. For my children's sake, I can no longer take the leap that would allow me to say all men are either practicing or latent batterers. My sons are good boys. Other mother's sons are also good boys and some of them are even grown-ups.

I am called upon daily to be empathetic to the opposite sex. It is a daunting but worthwhile challenge, and one that I believe was put to me because I needed the insights I have acquired. I've seen "part one" of my challenge almost through to completion. I am in the thick of things with "part two," and still beginning the journey with "part three." Each time I discover an effective parenting technique for Dan, I find it to be ineffective for the other two. They differ from each other as much as any three strangers on a bus differ. They mature at different rates, glom on to different hobbies, root for different teams, react in different ways to the same events. Bashing requires generalization and my sons cannot be generalized.

As a woman, I am astounded every day that I have helped create three men and live with four.

As a feminist, it is incumbent upon me to raise forthright, caring, respectful, egalitarian men.

As a mother, it is my dream that they will be all of those things plus exceedingly happy.

I want the world to greet them as the blessings they are. I want them to be judged by their own deeds and not pre-judged by the deeds of lesser men who preceded them. By desiring this, I owe it to the rest of their sex not to prejudge, not to generalize, not to bash.

I have given my sons to the world, and with this book, I have given my world to my sons. "You're all welcome."

Epilogue

Dear Daughter,

   With this letter I am letting you go. Your soul is free to choose another woman worthy of the blessing that is a daughter. I held you first as a dream. More than marriage or mortgage or menopause, I knew you were in my future. I saw your face in my mirror, freckled and fair. I named you Shira, which means song, and I sang to you, anticipating a lifetime of mother-daughter duets. And then I gave birth, only not to you, and I was weakened as much by surprise as by exertion. And you were no longer my dream. I named my dream baby Daniel and he was freckled and fair. He didn't like my singing. He liked for me to tell him stories about animals that could talk and boys that could slay giants. He moaned in ecstasy when he suckled at my breast, and later he would suck his thumb and twirl my hair, and I'm really sorry but I fell in love with him.

   I held you next as a hope. No longer vain enough to expect my dreams to be premonitions, I hoped as mortals do, knowing that I can control my destiny but not my miracles. I named you Madelaine, which is French, and I ate croissants and kept my eye on a little straw hat with a red ribbon. Even before café latté was fashionable, I hoped that we'd some day share some on the Rive Gauche. And then I gave birth, only not to you. Too afraid to be disappointed, I feigned utter joy. I named my baby of hope Andrew and he was born red and blue like the French flag. He didn't like my singing or my stories. He liked for me to take him for long walks, not along the Rive Gauche, but along the Delaware Canal. We walked and we walked and we watched the river freeze and thaw, and I'm really sorry but I fell in love with him too.

And finally I held you as a prayer. Totally humbled now, I prayed for one more blessing. I named you Ivy, and you were to be my salvation in old age. When your brothers fled to other women and faraway places, you would stay with me and talk with me and remind me that I was once young. Probably widowed because most women are, I would look to you for love and you, my daughter, would love me despite afflictions battling for possession of my memory.

My prayer was answered, but not by you. I named him Isaac and call him Zack, and I'll tell you before I tell you anything about him that I fell in love with him too.

He's unrefined lump sugar, and I eat him and drink him voraciously. He likes it when his brother Daniel tells him stories, and he likes it when his brother Andrew takes him for walks, and he likes it when I eat him and drink him.

I wasn't equipped for the journey I've been on. All of my tools and all of my plans were inappropriate. But I'm equipped now. I've improvised and I've made do and I've forged new paths. And I am happy.

I have to let you go so my friends with daughters will stop feeling sorry for me. I want to free them to share their stories and their glories without holding back out of a pity that I no longer need or want.

I have to let you go so my sons and my husband will know even more than they know already that *they* are my glory. They are my dreams, my hopes, my prayers.

I have a girl child. She is the girl inside of me who never grew up. The woman I have become has learned how to love her and nurture her, and I am teaching my boys how to do the same.

I have to let you go so you will be free to come into this world through a woman who needs you now more than I, a woman who may not be able to learn that a great piece of chocolate cake is as good as the best *mille-feuille* around. Come into the world, please, so your mother can love you and teach you to value and be valued by boys like mine.

Lots of kisses and good-bye.

About the Author

Photo by Gary Glassman

Karin Kasdin is an author and a playwright. Her plays in-
clude *Ten Triple A*, *Couples*, *Wallweeds*, and *Photo Finish*.
Her book, *Disaster Blasters: A Kid's Guide to Being Home
Alone*, was coauthored with Laura Szabo Cohen. She lives in
Bucks County, Pennsylvania, with her husband and three sons
whose lives are now an open book.